THE FIELDEN

A ramble through Todmorden's past

Jim Jarratt

Smith Settle

First published in 1988 by

Smith Settle
Ilkley Road
Otley
LS21 3JP

ISBN 1 870071 15 8

Frontispiece: the statue of 'Honest John' Fielden MP in Centre Vale park.
"This statue was raised by public subscription in gratitude to him
whose persevering efforts succeeded in obtaining the Ten Hours Act."

Designed, printed and bound by
SMITH SETTLE
Ilkley Road
Otley
LS21 3JP

THE FIELDEN TRAIL

Todmorden

Early Closing Day: Tuesday

Market Days: Wednesday, Friday and Saturday

Tourist Information: 1 Bridge Gate, Hebden Bridge
(Hebden Bridge 3831)

Railway Station: Leeds to Manchester line
(Todmorden 3488)

Bus Station: There are buses to Halifax, Burnley and Hebden Bridge
(Todmorden 2296)

Youth Hostel: Mankinholes village (Todmorden 2340)

Libraries: Todmorden Library, Rochdale Road (Todmorden 5600)
There are also branch libraries at Cornholme and Walsden

At the time of writing there are plans to open a Tourist Information
Centre in Todmorden in the summer of 1988

Contents

List of Photographs

List of Maps

To the memory of my granny, Mary Jarratt (formerly Mary Hattersley) who, like Mary Fielden, was also a manufacturer's daughter.

Acknowledgments

Thanks to the Librarian at Todmorden, the Town Council for permission to reproduce the Todmorden Coat of Arms, Pennine Heritage, Mrs Crabtree of The Mount and Mrs King of Hartley Royd, Mr Stansfield of Bottomley, and last, but by no means least, Kevin and Jane. Thanks for your patience Trish!

Introduction

In the autumn of 1983 I had never even heard of the Fieldens of Todmorden. Perhaps the name may once have rung faintly at the back of my mind in connection with the 'O' Level History classes of far off schooldays; but if it ever did, it had certainly been consigned to oblivion long ago. Even if I had, in the course of my casual reading ever encountered the name, I would never have thought of it as the potential subject for a book.

On 19th January 1984 I was chatting with one of my neighbours in Mytholmroyd, Kevin Hoyle. He knew of my interest in local history and told me that he had temporarily acquired some old papers from an acquaintance, papers that I might perhaps find interesting? The material, he informed me, related to the Fielden Family of Todmorden, who were local manufacturers. I was interested, though more casually than seriously, and told him that I would certainly like to have a look at the stuff, even though the Fieldens and their world were quite unknown to me.

That evening he presented me with a rather battered looking manilla envelope crammed full of old papers. Some were older than others, the most venerable of them being a parchment dating from the reign of James I, an indenture referring to a marriage settlement involving one Ralph Elmston, yeoman of Kent. Here was treasure indeed! This parchment, however, proved to be the odd one out, for, with the sole exception of an 18th century copy of 'The Spectator', all the other documents were connected with the radical political movements of the early 19th century, The 'Ten Hours' Movement and the Fieldens. For the most part, the papers were political pamphlets produced by the Lancashire Central Short Time Committee, usually referring to the efforts of John Fielden M.P. in attempting to obtain a 'Ten Hours Bill'. There was a copy of Cobbett's Political Register, and various tracts on various subjects published by John Fielden's sons. But most interesting of all were the letters, which (with the sole exception of one written by Samuel Fielden whilst in Liverpool) were all written by John Fielden's second daughter, Mary, mainly to her brother John, who was at boarding school in Liverpool at the time (1836).

Not long after receiving these papers I mentioned them to my sister-in-law Esther, who had recently completed an 'O' Level History course at Bradford College. I was surprised to find that she had not only heard of the Fieldens, but wished dearly that she could have had access to material such as this when she was on the course! 'Did I not know' she informed me, 'that John Fielden was an M.P. and a famous radical reformer, a champion of the workers who fought to improve working conditions in factories and mines?' John Fielden was, I was soon to discover, far more than just a mere manufacturer; I was indeed surprised to find out that the tatty looking envelope contained material of immense historical interest.

I quickly realised that all this material belonged in a public record office, and not in a battered envelope in someone's bottom drawer. Here was an untapped source of local history of potential historical value. I later discovered that not even the local libraries could provide all of the pamphlets that were in this little hoard. And as for the letters - they were irreplaceable!

After a month or so of photocopying and recording information contained in the papers, I decided that it was about time I returned them to their rightful owner. I gave them to Kevin, who duly returned them. Shortly afterwards, Kevin, who worked at an old folks home in Rochdale, left his job; and when, sometime later, in the throes of writing The Fielden Trail I asked him for the name of his mysterious 'acquaintance' who lent him the papers, I was stunned to find that he could not remember!

I can but hope that the papers (wherever they are) will eventually resurface and find their way into local archives, where they can be well looked after and further studied by anyone wishing to further explore the history of the Fieldens of Todmorden. The Librarian at Todmorden would particularly like to see the papers, and I can only hope that if this book catches the attention of their owner, he will see fit to come forward and take steps to protect these interesting documents from further deterioration.

So it was that Mary Fielden's letters left my life as mysteriously as they had entered it. But she had done her work: in me she had kindled an interest in finding out about her and the great and influential family of which she was a part. With old maps and a notebook I laced up my boots and set off in search of the Fieldens of Todmorden. The result of that quest is this book.

Jim Jarratt

Mytholmroyd
1988

xii

About The Fielden Trail

Sometime in the middle of the 16th century one William Fielden, yeoman farmer, married and set up house at Inchfield, a remote farmstead in the Walsden Valley, deep in the Pennines. From such humble beginnings sprang a family who were to play a major role in the social and economic development of the Upper Calder Valley; whilst one of their number, 'Honest John' Fielden, was destined to make his name in parliament as a champion of the labouring classes, thus entering the name of Fielden into the annals of the nation's history.

In this book you will walk through town and countryside, through urban bustle and through wild and lonely places where the wind howls through shattered walls and tumbled stones. You will discover the Fieldens: who they were, where they lived and how they lived. You will also see how Todmorden grew from a small hamlet to an industrial mill town; you will see the coming of the mills, the canals, the railways, riots and revelations, rough-hewn hillfolk seeking salvation — and the right to vote. You will see how the Fieldens and the story of Todmorden are inseperable — nothing of any note ever happened in Todmorden without there being a Fielden around to witness it. In finding the Fieldens you will also discover the history of Todmorden.

Like Phyllis Bentley's Inheritance, The Fielden Trail traces the rise of a family of 'mill magnates', but with a difference - the people and places presented in this book are real! Todmorden and its surrounding districts was (and still is) 'home' to the Fieldens, who, unlike most textile barons, preferred to live near their workers and built their great houses nearby, rather than moving away to more genteel parts. Because of this, we are given the rare opportunity of being able to trace back their story through generation after generation without moving from the Todmorden area. In a day's ramble we can stroll through time and space, saunter through the centuries and visualise the whole panoply of Upper Calderdale's history through the eyes of one family — the Fieldens — who, even if they did not entirely bring about the development of Todmorden into a modern community certainly bore witness to all of it.

The Fielden Trail is a thematic history trail. It is not, however, a journey that involves an afternoon's gentle stroll around the 'sights' of Todmorden. On the contrary, it is a tough hike of some 19 miles or more involving a lot of repeated ascent and as much descent. Section 1 to Cornholme and Sections 2 and 3 to Dawson Weir and Rake End follow the upland shelf for much of the way, but Section 4 takes to the high moors, following a route which involves some rough going along the high moorland ridge between Gaddings and Stoodley Pike, not a journey to be undertaken badly-equipped in inclement weather (which is the norm rather than the exception at Stoodley Pike!). I have divided the walk into sections intentionally, the end of each section providing an easy escape route back to the centre of Todmorden. Thus it is possible to walk the Fielden Trail in sections as a leisurely ramble, or in its entirety as a tough challenge walk. In the early days of planning the Fielden Trail, I had great doubts about the possibility of such a route. It seemed that merely connecting locations with Fielden associations would not give me a walk that made any geographical (or historical) sense; but yet, as I researched my subject more deeply, I found that pieces of a puzzle have a habit of falling into place exactly where you want them to fall.

The geography of the Fielden Trail is fascinating. Unlike many walks, you finish up almost where you started, so this is a walk for motorists. Todmorden lies at the confluence of two rivers and three valleys: the Fielden Trail follows the edges of all three valleys, creating a walk that constantly winds back upon itself, as if one were walking around 'The Legs of Man'. By the time you have walked the Fielden Trail you will know the topography of the Todmorden area quite intimately, having viewed Todmorden from virtually every point of the compass. Even if you aren't the slightest bit interested in the Fieldens and find history boring (like my wife!) you'll find it's still worth doing just for the walk. Study or challenge, history or hike, you will find the Fielden Trail physically and mentally stimulating, walking through hill and dale, town and countryside, past and present.

The Fielden Trail is an arduous walk of almost 20 miles. Those undertaking it as a 'challenge walk' are strongly advised to prepare well. Stout boots, food and waterproofs are necessary, particularly on the upland sections.

Follow the Country Code. Do not leave litter, climb walls or disturb livestock. Leave gates as you find them, beware of fires and keep dogs under control.

The maps in this book should be used in conjunction with a suitable Ordnance Survey map, eg the South Pennines 1:25000.

Map Key

The maps in this book are not to scale

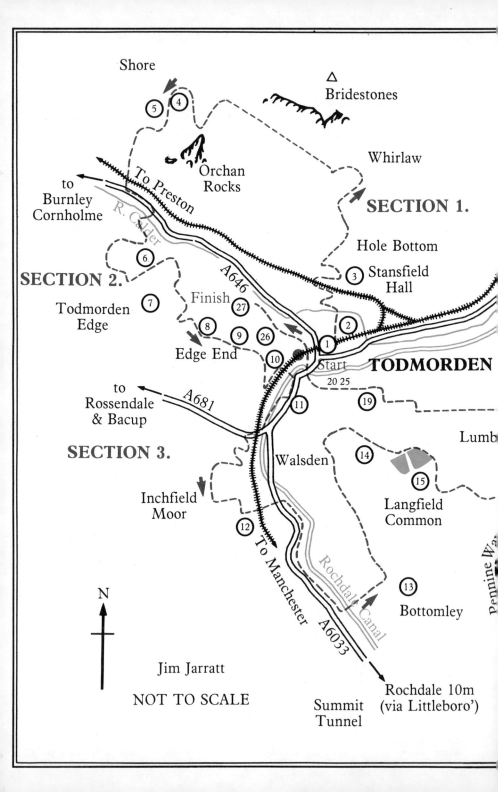

The Fielden Trail

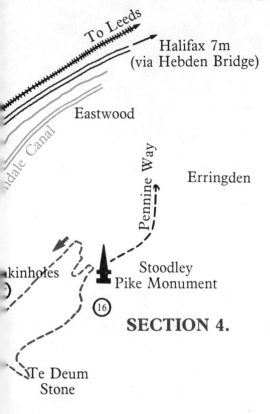

To Leeds

Halifax 7m
(via Hebden Bridge)

Eastwood

Pennine Way

Erringden

Calderdale Canal

kinholes

Stoodley
Pike Monument

16

SECTION 4.

Te Deum
Stone

Key

1.	Todmorden Town Hall	15.	Gaddings Reservoir
2.	Site of Roomfield School	16.	Stoodley Pike Monument
3.	Stansfield Hall	17.	Mankinholes
4.	Hartley Royd	18.	Lumbutts
5.	Mercer Field	19.	Shoebroad Burial Ground
6.	Robin Wood Mill	20.	Todmorden Unitarian Church
7.	Todmorden Edge	21.	Sunday School
8.	Edge End Farm	22.	Golden Lion
9.	Dobroyd Castle	23.	Conservative Club
10.	Dawson Weir	24.	Todmorden Hall
11.	Waterside	25.	White Harte
12.	Inchfield	26	Carr Laithe
13.	Bottomley	27.	John Fielden's Statue
14.	Basin Stone		

SECTION 1

Cornholme via West Whirlaw, Orchan Rocks and Hartley Royd

The trail starts at Todmorden Town Hall and finishes by the statue of John Fielden in Centre Vale Park, a mere ten minutes walk away. Between these two points however, you have got around 19 miles of hike to tackle, some of it over rough terrain. So gird up your loins and let's get going, to the start of Section 1 of the Fielden Trail at:-

Todmorden Town Hall

Having got off the bus, parked your car, or whatever, pause a moment to admire the magnificent yet petite edifice of Todmorden Town Hall. Designed in 1870 by John Gibson, it is in the classical style with a semicircular northern end, and is also endowed with fine statuary expressing the history of Todmorden on its southern-facing pediment. It cost around £54,000, and was built at the expense of Samuel, John and Joshua Fielden; it was opened by Lord John Manners on 3rd April 1875, along with the unveiling of their father 'Honest John's' statue, which stood on the western side of the Town Hall before setting off on its travels. Prior to 1888 the county boundary ran through the middle of the Town Hall, and this is indicated on the pediment (the river also flows beneath the Town Hall).

Firmly embedded in the ground the Town Hall may be — not so 'Honest John' Fielden, with whom we have a distant appointment in Centre Vale Park. So lace up your boots, check your watch and we'll be off! St. Mary's Church, opposite the Town Hall, was probably founded by the Radcliffes between 1400 and 1476. If you can spare the time at this stage, give it a visit. The East Window commemorates Mr. John Fielden J.P. of Dobroyd Castle, whose widow presented oak screens in 1904.

Now turn right through the market place to the Market Hall, opened in 1879, its foundation stone laid by the Fieldens. If it's a market day you will see some of the hurly-burly and bustle of this independent little border town, which, as you will soon discover, has a charm and character all of its own which is not always immediately apparent.

When I began the walk, the hardware shop at the front of the Market Hall had a handwritten notice which boasted 'DONKEY STONES ARE IN STOCK'. Here is a piece of social history in one phrase: once, in an age of rows of back-to-back mill workers' houses and cobbled streets, whitening your doorstep with a donkey stone was obligatory, and heaven help anyone who didn't bother to 'donkey' their front step — they were sent to Coventry by the rest of the street! Who says 'keeping up with the Joneses' is a modern phenomenon?

To the right of the Market Hall is a public convenience, and a large open parking area, on the site of what was formerly streets and rows of

Todmorden Town Hall.

houses. Nearby is the recently constructed Todmorden Health Centre, and beyond it a block of flats — Roomfield House (you may have seen it in an episode of 'Juliet Bravo' which is filmed around here). Nearby stood:-

Roomfield School

This was the first Board School in Todmorden, opened in 1878. (The remains of the playground walls can still be seen around the flats.) The Fielden Trail does not visit Roomfield House (there is nothing to see) but instead crosses the little footbridge over the river behind the Market Hall. Pause on the bridge a moment and listen to the following harrowing tale from the statement of Henrietta Shepherd to her son Levi, concerning the brave deed for which her husband James Shepherd was awarded a testimonial and a silver medal from the Royal Humane Society:

"On the 14th August 1891 there was a terrible flood. The River Calder was in full spate, and [downstream of Todmorden] was running level with the canal, forming huge lakes across the valley. Here, at Roomfield, the school was flooded and children had to be rescued from the school. To do this, long planks were put across weft boxes to form a bridge, for the children to cross over. Whilst the children were walking on these planks, one little boy, Samuel S. Fielden, fell into the roaring river and was quickly washed out of sight.

At Springside [about 2½ miles downstream] people had been alerted about the accident, and were watching the river for a sight of the boy. One of these people, James Shepherd, Foreman Dyer at Moss Bros. Springside, saw the boy in the river and immediately jumped into the river, and reached the boy. Being a powerful swimmer, he managed to get the boy to the side of the river near Callis. Here help was at hand to pull them out. The boy was badly bruised by his rough journey down the river, and only survived a few hours. James Shepherd was none the worse for his ordeal. The courage of this man must be appreciated, when you realise that he had a wife and seven children at home. The youngest, twins, were just two months old.

Later James Shepherd was presented with his testimonial and silver medal. On the face of the medal is engraved:-
'Presented to Mr. James Shepherd.'
On the reverse:- 'For saving Samuel S. Fielden from the River Calder, 14th August 1891. Presented with a testimonial from the Royal Humane Society for his bravery.'

The Fielden family also presented him with a new suit of clothes for the one ruined in the river. In one of the pockets was a gold sovereign."

So, as you stare at this babbling little brook and try to envisage what kind of a flood it must have been that could sweep a little boy to his death, cross the footbridge (it has steel rails in a trellis pattern, and crosses the river behind the Market Hall, just below the meeting of the Calder with its Walsden tributary), pass behind the Bus Station, (the river flows between concrete walls here and the buses turn on the far side), and go under the railway viaduct, which carries the railway at a high level over the rooftops of Todmorden. Todmorden Viaduct carries the Manchester line over nine arches, seven of them with a sixty foot span, 54½ feet above the road. The railway was opened on March 1st 1841, and Thomas Fielden, who was one of the railway company directors, proved to be a thorn in the flesh of the board's chairman on more than one occasion, as we shall see.

Beyond the viaduct, cross waste ground by a garage to emerge by a fish and chip shop. Here turn right down Stansfield Road. High on the hillside to the right can be seen the tower of Cross Stone Church, which has Brontë associations. It was originally built centuries ago to cater for the needs of upland farmers, being rebuilt in 1714, pulled down, and re-erected in 1835. It is presently in a ruinous condition. The Brontë sisters stayed at Cross Stone Vicarage in September 1829.

Now continue onwards, bearing gradually to the left. Soon Stansfield Road joins Wellington Road, coming up from the left. Turn right and pass across a footbridge over the railway, passing a YEB installation on the left to emerge on Stansfield Hall Road near its junction with Woodlands Avenue. Bear right and soon a small road appears on the left, by a ginnel with steps, signed 'To The Hollins', close by the entrance gates to:-

Stansfield Hall

The Fielden Trail bears left up the hill towards 'The Hollins', but before continuing onwards, follow the road on to the right for a short distance, in order to get a peek at Stansfield Hall, a fine mansion by John Gibson. The older building at the far side is the original Stansfield Hall, which in its turn was built on the site of a still older house. 'Honest John's' three sons each built mansions for themselves around Todmorden, and Stansfield Hall was the residence of the youngest son, Joshua Fielden, who was born in 1827.

Todmorden to Cornholme

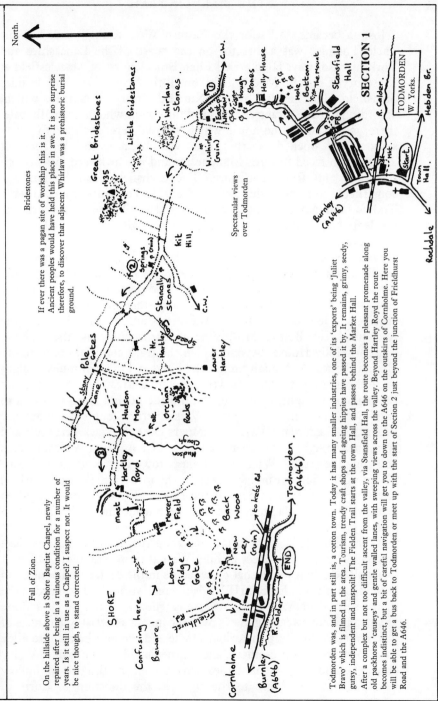

North.

Bridestones

If ever there was a pagan site of worship this is it. Ancient peoples would have held this place in awe. It is no surprise therefore, to discover that adjacent Whirlaw was a prehistoric burial ground.

Fall of Zion.

On the hillside above is Shore Baptist Chapel, newly repaired after being in a ruinous condition for a number of years. Is it still in use as a Chapel? I suspect not. It would be nice though, to stand corrected.

Spectacular views over Todmorden

SECTION 1

TODMORDEN
W. Yorks.

Great Bridestones

Little Bridestones.

435

Whirlaw Stones.

Kit Hill.

Springs

Stanally Stones

Lower Hartley

Stony Pole Lane

Hudson Moor.

Mt. Hartley

Orchan Rocks

Hudson Clough

Hartley Royd.

mast

Mercer Field

Back Wood

New Ley (ruin)

Lower Ridge Gate

Confusing here Beware!

SHORE

Cornholme
Burnley (A646)

R. Calder.

Frieldhurst Rd.

to Robs Rd.

Todmorden (A646)

END

W. Whirlaw (ruin)

East Whirlaw

Hough Stones

Holly House

Hole Bottom

The Mount

Stansfield Hall.

Start.

Town Hall.

Burnley (A646)

R. Calder.

Rochdale

Hebden Br.

Todmorden was, and in part still is, a cotton town. Today it has many smaller industries, one of its 'exports' being 'Juliet Bravo' which is filmed in the area. Tourism, trendy craft shops and ageing hippies have passed it by. It remains, grimy, seedy, gutsy, independent and unspoilt! The Fielden Trail starts at the town Hall, and passes behind the Market Hall.

After a complex but not too difficult ascent from the valley, via Stansfield Hall, the route becomes a pleasant promenade along old packhorse 'causeys' and gentle walled lanes, with sweeping views across the valley. Beyond Hartley Royd the route becomes indistinct, but a bit of careful navigation will get you to down to the A646 on the outskirts of Cornholme. Here you will be able to get a bus back to Todmorden or meet up with the start of Section 2 just beyond the junction of Frieldhurst Road and the A646.

Joshua became M.P. for the Eastern West Riding, and, like his uncle Thomas, was a director on the board of the Lancashire and Yorkshire Railway. He married Ellen Brocklehurst of Macclesfield at Prestbury Church, Macclesfield on 14th May 1851, and besides Stansfield Hall he also owned Nutfield Priory in Surrey, which, according to Mrs. Crabtree, my local informant who has actually been there, is not unlike the house which you see here. In 1869 a railway station was opened nearby; this was because the junction at Todmorden faced towards Manchester and was awkward for through traffic to and from Yorkshire. The Stansfield Hall Station was constructed to remedy this fault and enable Yorkshire trains to serve Todmorden. No trace of it remains today. Of course the original residents of Stansfield Hall were the Stansfields, who we will shortly encounter, although at a much earlier period in time.

From the gates of Stansfield Hall, bear left up the road past The Hollins. This passes The Hollins (below crags) and also Willow Bank. Beyond a row of red brick houses the road narrows into a path for a few yards then widens out again, passing stone houses on the left to emerge at Hole Bottom Road. Ahead lies an old mill chimney (the remains of Hole Bottom Mill). Where the track forks take the left hand route to Holly House, beyond which the track continues onwards to Hough Stones. At Hough Stones the Fielden Trail continues straight on, following a path under hawthorns with a stream on the left. Soon the path bears right, ascending the hillside behind Hough Stones to enter Scrapers Lane, to the left of Wickenberry Clough. Turn left and follow the Calderdale Way. At Scrapers Gate the track bears left and continues straight on between walls. On the left is East Whirlaw Farm and on the right Whirlaw Stones, towering ominously above Todmorden, dominating the skyline. Soon a ruin (West Whirlaw) appears on the left and beyond the gate the route becomes a paved 'causey' over moorland, contouring the hillside among boulders and cotton grass.

By the ruins of West Whirlaw is a good spot to break out the flask and sandwiches and reflect awhile. We have now entered a different world. The urban world that crowded us in the centre of Todmorden is suddenly a vain illusion. HERE is the real world. In Todmorden the moors seem distant; here the reverse is true. If the day be clear there are magnificent sweeping views over the moors and vast open tracts of wild country, dwarfing the urban smoke and clamour below. Stoodley Pike Monument is prominent, and on the far side of the Calder Valley above Todmorden, Mankinholes can be seen, nestling in its hollow below the moors. More to the right in the direction of Burnley,

Todmorden Edge can be seen as a cluster of houses hugging the opposite hillside as if wearing a woolly overcoat against the bleak winter weather. Below in the valley is Todmorden, where the start of the walk can be clearly seen.

If the world below us is modern, then the world above us dwells at the opposite pole. Whirlaw is an ancient prehistoric burial ground, and the strange contorted rocks of the Bridestones, weird and mysterious in mist, are an obvious pagan site. Indeed they offer the appearance of a natural Stonehenge. No ancient man could visit such a place as this without being inspired to awe and worship. The ancient aura seems to linger in the name 'Scrapers Lane', which also suggests to me, like the place-name 'Flints' at Crow Hill Sowerby, that ancient artefacts have been found here in more recent times.

Stansfield Hall, former residence of Joshua Fielden MP.

As you pack your flask and continue onwards over open moor, the feeling of close proximity to the past becomes more intense. The landscape has changed, and has become more austere, more primitive. Todmorden, like most mill towns in the Upper Calder Valley, appears like a distant oasis of bustle and worldly activity far below. In winter it is flood-prone, yet relatively sheltered, and in summer it appears green and lush. Yet up here, on the upland shelf between the valley floor and the high moors, the real nature of the landscape becomes instantly apparent.

Here time has stood still. The prehistoric worshippers, the legions of Rome, they all departed long ago. In their wake came English, Norsemen and Danes, the first hill farmers, clearing the land, claiming rough pastures from the inhospitable hills, felling the ancient birch forests, digging peat, building farmsteads and laithes, keeping livestock, and, perhaps most significantly of all, carding, spinning and weaving woollen cloth. No doubt there were ancestors of the Fieldens among these people, not to mention the Stansfields, Greenwoods, Radcliffes and various other ancient families indigenous to the Upper Calder Valley.

In the wake of the farmers (and in some cases before them) came the arteries of communication, the drove roads and packhorse ways; and, walking on the old causey stones below the Bridestones and Whirlaw, we might, in this quiet solitude, almost hear the jingle of packhorse bells. 'Long Causeways', ancient boundary stones and wayside crosses all abound in this area. Are they Tudor, Mediaeval, or Viking — perhaps even older? No-one knows. English history went its schoolbook way: red rose fought white, the monasteries were dissolved, first the Renaissance and then the Reformation swept Europe; yet right here, in these bleak northern uplands, we might still be in ancient times, such is the scarcity of information relating to this area as it was in those far-off days.

High above the valley floor on this upland shelf, what civilisation there was in the Upper Calder Valley first developed. (The valleys were marshy and thickly wooded.) From this level, with the advent of the Industrial Revolution in the late 18th century, the pattern of development was to move downhill, building factories and towns, leaving solitude and desolation in its wake as the surge towards progress, industry and improved communications led embryonic industrialists like the Fieldens to abandon the stony places of their youth, and become dwellers in, and builders of, large industrial townships like Todmorden.

Up here, in the shadow of rock outcrops and moors, is where the

Fieldens (and many families like them) began, eking out a harsh living from bleak upland pastures. Down in the valley is where they went to make their fortunes, and back to the countryside (in gentler climes) is where they returned afterwards to build their great houses, returning not as poor yeoman farmers, but as influential landowners, weighted with honours and privileges.

Walking amongst rough-hewn ruins on bleak hillsides we are now at the beginning of our trail of inheritance. Through these upland pastures (and very likely along this ancient packhorse way) sometime in the middle of the 16th century came Nicholas Fielden, yeoman farmer of Inchfield in the Parish of Rochdale. His father, William Fielden, was also a farmer, though his roots are rather less clear, it being uncertain as to whether he came from Leventhorpe near Bradford, or Heyhouses near Sabden.

Whatever his roots, however, the business that brought Nicholas Fielden so far from his own home in the adjacent Walsden Valley to these bleak Whirlaw uplands is quite clear: he came as a suitor. On this side of the Calder Valley dwelt Christobel, daughter of John Stansfield of Stansfield, and Nicholas eventually married her. Whether or not Nicholas and Christobel walked hand-in-hand along these hillsides, the wind in their hair, or were merely the unwilling victims of their parents' dynastic ambitions, we can only speculate. One thing we do know is that their marriage, arranged or not, was fruitful, and we must hope that they were happy together.

As a result of this union, the farms of Hartley Royd and Mercerfield (which we are shortly to visit) passed to Nicholas' children, of which he had five (four sons and a daughter), before Christobel died sometime after 1582. Nicholas remarried, taking as his second wife Elizabeth Greenwood, who, in 1638 was described as 'living at Inchfield aged' (Nicholas having died in 1626). Whether or not Nicholas' children acquired these Calderdale estates as a result of their mother's inheritance or marriage settlement is uncertain, but it seems likely, as there would appear to be no record of any Fieldens living on this side of the valley prior to this period, which suggests that the lands originally belonged to the Stansfields.

Unfortunately the picture of the Fieldens in the 16th and early 17th centuries is not as straightforward as this. The Fieldens of Inchfield (and later Shore, Hartley Royd and Mercerfield) were not the only family of that name living in the vicinity of what was eventually to become Todmorden. On the opposite side of the Walsden Valley to Inchfield, at Bottomley, another family of Fieldens was firmly established. Whether or not they were cousins to Nicholas' family is not clear. One thing is certain however: in the near future a Fielden was going to marry another Fielden and from this union was to spring that branch of the Fielden family with which this book is concerned.

From West Whirlaw the causey passes over the moor amongst boulders and heather, beneath Whirlaw and the Bridestones, which dominate the horizon on the right. After a succession of metal gates the path becomes a 'green lane' running between walls. Continue to the next iron gate, just beyond which the Calderdale Way branches off to the left, down to Rake Hey Farm and Todmorden. Ignore this route, instead continuing onwards along Stoney Lane, passing trees and ruined farm buildings (named 'Springs' on the 1844 map). Keep going and soon, after a gentle rise, the lane reaches a junction of paths at Pole Gates.

Here a choice must be made. Do not follow the lane onwards, but pass through the gate to the left. From here an indistinct path bears to the right over Hudson Moor to Hudson Bridge and Hartley Royd. Most walkers, however, will be tempted to follow the farm track down to Orchan Rocks. After all, you will argue, I've talked at length about strange rocks and pagan rituals, but I haven't taken my route to any of them! Well now's your chance: Orchan Rocks are not very far off-route, and visiting them is well worth the necessary detour, so, just to make you happy, I'll take my main route that way!

The way is quite obvious. Follow the track downhill and then cut across open moorland until you arrive at the Orchan Rocks. Here another place to break out the flask and sandwiches. If you can stand the 'airiness' of the situation there are superb views over the gorge below. Many names are carved on the slabs, although I could find no Fieldens among them when I was there. The Fieldens would have known this spot however, and, like us, would no doubt have marvelled at its strangeness.

From Orchan Rocks bear right over Hudson Moor. Soon, near some quarrying remains, a distinct path is met with, and Hartley Royd can be seen on the far side of Hudson Clough. Follow the path to Hudson Bridge, then continue onwards, finally entering the Hartley Royd farm road through an iron gate. Turn left to arrive at:-

Hartley Royd

In 1624 Nicholas Fielden of Inchfield (whom we have recently encountered) made out his last will and testament, which divided his property amongst his children. To his eldest son John he bequeathed "ffurther Shore" and a moiety (or part) of Mercerfield. Hartley Royd must have been included in this package, for in his own will John Fielden is described as 'John ffeilden of Hartley Royd, Stansfield in the County of York, Yeoman." The second son, Abraham, inherited Inchfield, and his eldest son, John, also lived at Hartley Royd. Abraham married Elizabeth Fielden of Bottomley, thus uniting two branches of Fieldens, and it is this line whose fortunes we are to follow throughout most of this book. This Abraham Fielden was 'Honest John' Fielden's great, great, great grandfather.

But back to Hartley Royd. Further Shore passed to Nicholas' third son, Joshua, and the other half of Mercerfield went to the youngest, Anthonie. Confused? You soon will be! How, you will ask, does all this relate to the mullioned farmhouse that stands before us? Did John Fielden build the place? The first thing you will notice is the ornate datestone in the north wall, then you will try to read it, but its very serpentine ornateness makes it difficult to decipher. Oh dear, it's in Latin! At this point I was lucky enough to receive the assistance of Mrs. King, the farmer's wife. She said that people often tried to decipher the inscription, so much so that her son had been prompted to sit down one day and find out what it actually did say. It reads as follows:-

JOHN FIELDEN AND WIFE ELIZABETH
FROM HARM AT HOME 1724.

Simple eh? No it's not — the date's wrong! The John Fielden we have been talking about died in 1645. This must be a later descendant, and referring to Fishwick's genealogy of the Fieldens only brings more confusion. Our "John ffeilden of Hartley Royd, Yeoman" had a son called John who "inherited his father's lands with the remainder to *his* son John" (my italics). This second John would have been at least 79 years old in 1724 so it seems likely that it was a third John, the grandson, who carved the datestone and presumably built the present house. I say 'confusing' because the same genealogy also speaks of another "John ffeilden of Hartley Royd", son of Abraham and Elizabeth Fielden. He is named in Elizabeth Fielden's will in 1673, and in accordance with his father's will conveyed Bottomley to his brother Joshua. *His* will is dated 14th February 1679!

One possible way of easing this sort of confusion is to realise that these wills are referring to land parcels and not to particular residences. The first John Fielden was "of Hartley Royd", yet he owned "ffurther Shore" and part of Mercerfield. To farm it you did not necessarily have to live on it, and the Fieldens owned patches of land all over the place, houses being divided up amongst relatives, and new pastures being acquired by marriage. Eventually we reach a point where we have to speculate: the John Fielden who was Abraham's eldest son had two sons who inherited lands, Joshua of Swineshead and Nicholas of Shore. Neither of these could have been "from harm at home" at Hartley Royd in 1724, so I am led to conclude that it must have been the third John mentioned earlier who raised the datestone.

Looking at Hartley Royd raises more speculations. If this house was indeed built in 1724, what of the earlier house? The style of the present building with its mullioned windows and externally protruding chimneybreast is more evocative of the 17th than the 18th century. This fact leads us to two possible conclusions. Either the house was built in 1724 in a style which by that time was going out of fashion (this is by no means unlikely as Pennine hill farms were

Hartley Royd from Hudson Bridge.

severely functional in design and styles were a lot slower to change
than they were in more 'civilised' areas), or the house was built in the
17th century and underwent alterations in 1724 which resulted in the
datestone we now see. And a final question: irrespective of when the
present house was built, was there an earlier, perhaps Tudor, house on
the site? Or an even older one perhaps? We do not know, we can only
speculate.

In 1648 George Fox began public work in Manchester, and William
Dewsbury probably preached around Todmorden in 1653. In 1654
John Fielden of Inchfield and Joshua Fielden of Bottomley were
reported as being Quakers. By association with his brother Joshua, it is
apparent that this John Fielden is the same one who is referred to in
the genealogy as being "of Hartley Royd" who "conveyed Bottomley
to his brother Joshua". If he lived at Inchfield — his father Abraham
did, and John was his eldest son — that should clarify further the
mystery of who lived at Hartley Royd.

John suffered for his Quaker faith: in 1665 he was fined for not
attending church and as he declined to pay, a cheese was taken off him
and sold for 4s. 6d. Three years later he suffered 31 weeks
imprisonment for non-attendance, whilst the following year five of his
oxen were seized and sold (at a value of £23) and he himself spent eight
weeks in jail at Preston. His brother Joshua was buried at Shoebroad
on his death in 1693.

John died in 1698, but there is no mention of his resting place.
There is another Quaker burial ground at Todmorden Edge, and Mrs
King informed me that at Shore there is a field called "t'Quaker
Pasture". Quakers were not allowed any monuments or gravestones,
so their burial grounds arc not immediately apparent. Perhaps
somewhere in "t'Quaker Pasture" at Shore lie the mortal remains of
"John ffeilden of Inchfield and Hartley Royd, Yeoman."

Before visiting Todmorden Edge, and another chapter in the
Fielden story, we visit Mercerfield and reflect awhile. From Hartley
Royd follow the track that leads through the farmyard towards the
valley. Just beyond the farm buildings another more recent track leads
down to a TV booster mast (leastways that's what I think it is). Just
beyond is an iron field gate in a wall. Do not pass through it, instead
follow the wall to the right. The wall soon becomes a fence running
even more sharply to the right, and Shore Baptist Chapel can be seen
on the hillside opposite. At the bottom of the slope a stile enters a
dilapidated track coming down from Ridge Gate. Turn left, and pass
through an old gate to the barn at:-

Mercerfield

Only the barn remains, and a rusty old fence straddles the ruins of what once was the house. There is an old door lintel here but the inscription is quite illegible, being badly eroded. The nearest I could get was:

H E C . . . 17 . . .

On the other side of the fence is a more legible stone with the date 1829. Mercerfield was divided between Nicholas and Christobel Fielden's sons John and Anthonie. It seems unlikely that there was a house here in the early 17th century, but there is no way we can be sure. If there was a house here in those far-off days, it must have been a tiny one judging by the ruins of the more recent house.

Here at Mercerfield, tucked snugly on its hillside in a hollow beneath the TV mast, with fine views down the gorge to Cornholme and its mills, is a place to sit down, break out the coffee and let your thoughts wander. Hartley Royd was a fine house, but it was also a farmyard, alive and kicking, fraught with canine menace and bovine sanctity, hardly conducive to flights of fantasy. Here, sitting amongst the pathetic ruins of Mercerfield we are alone with the hills, and we can, beset on all sides with Johns and Joshuas, try to find some clarity in the murky confusion. We can travel in time and try to get a picture of what life must have been like for those yeomen farmers and their families.

What a different world it must have been for those early Fieldens. Nicholas Fielden's grandfather was alive in the reign of Henry VIII. He would have lived through the dissolution of the monasteries, the Pilgrimage of Grace, and would have witnessed some of the repercussions of these events. Life must have been harsh, austere and uncomfortable in those turbulent times. Houses were cold and draughty, and lighting poor or non-existent. The noble 17th century farmsteads and clothier's houses we see on the hillsides today belong to a later generation of housing, born of a minor revolution in techniques of quarrying and stoneworking. Tudor houses in the Pennines were timber framed, often with walls of lath, wattle and daub rather than stone, and smokeholes in the roof rather than sophisticated flues and chimney stacks. Cruck houses, built with skills and techniques passed down from Norse settlers, were common, so backward was this remote upland area. Earthen floors and log fires — these are the kind of houses the Fieldens' mediaeval forebears would have known. The only towns of any note were York, Lancaster and

London, and they were far away, almost in another world.

Nicholas Fielden's grandchildren would not have found life too comfortable either. Their homes, though more embattled and sturdy, would have been every bit as uncomfortable. They would keep livestock on these bleak pastures and supplement a meagre living by producing woollen cloth to be sold at the nearest market, probably Heptonstall. Later, merchants and middlemen would become involved as the domestic textile industry developed, but at this early stage it would have been every man working for himself.

John and Joshua Fielden, Nicholas' grandchildren, were persecuted for their nonconformist beliefs. They lived through the great Civil War, and were no doubt aware of — if not actually involved with — the skirmish "ovver t'hill" at Heptonstall between the Parliamentarian garrison there and Mackworth's Royalists, who marched out of Halifax only to be repulsed by crashing boulders and fast-flowing waters. They might also have witnessed the garrison's departure over the moors into Lancashire (perhaps along the very packhorse route that runs above Hartley Royd) and heard reports of the sacking and burning of Heptonstall by the Royalists. Perhaps, with their Puritan beliefs, they wondered if their familes might next be ravaged and put to the sword? As Quakers their sympathies would have no doubt lain with the Parliamentary cause, even if their faith forbade them to take up arms.

The only thing we do know is that they survived these turbulent times — probably by minding their own business. Poor hillfarmers like the Fieldens would have little to offer the foraging armies of the Civil Wars. Indeed then, as now, the whole area would have been hostile to people in search of shelter and wholesome food. Good food came from the rich farming areas of the lowlands; the high hills and moors of the Pennines were only good for sheep farming and rough pastures. In the war, food supplies from the arable lowlands would have been cut to virtually a trickle, forcing up prices and bringing privation and hunger to the hillfolk of the Pennines, who eked out a living by selling their cloth. Times must have been hard indeed.

However, the sound of a train coming up the valley towards Cornholme breaks our reverie and we are back to the present day. Other Fieldens and other centuries await us, so we must say goodbye to the Fieldens of Shore, and push on up the other side of the valley towards Todmorden Edge. As you descend towards the bottom of the valley, make a good note of the topography of the opposite hillside if you intend continuing beyond Section 1. The path, zigzagging up the hillside opposite to a ruined farm on the edge of the moor, is the way

Cornholme from Mercer Field.

out from the gorge and the first part of Section 2 of the Fielden Trail.

From Mercerfield the route is indistinct and there is a multiplicity of sheep paths. The object is to get down to New Ley, a tiny little farmhouse in a ruinous condition, surrounded by nettles. The roof is starting to collapse now, but its size and interior give a pretty good idea of what Mercerfield must have been like when it was standing. For that reason alone, it is worth stopping for a moment.

From New Ley an enclosed path leads down to another ruined farm with green painted lintels, where it joins a track coming in from the left. The track descends towards a bungalow near some red brick houses, to emerge into Frieldhurst Road. Turn left and pass under the railway line to emerge into the main Burnley Road.

This is the end of Section 1. If you are not continuing onto Section 2 this is the place to catch a bus back to Todmorden. On foot it is a long walk down a busy road, but if the hour is late, this is preferable to following Section 2, which involves some awkward countryside and a lot of ascent, not very enjoyable in bad weather. I'd catch the bus if I was you, you can always tackle Section 2 on another day when you feel up to it. Don't worry about it, we'll go on our own!

SECTION 2

Waterside via Wet Shaw, Todmorden Edge, Edge End and Dobroyd Castle

If you are starting here you will have to get the Burnley bus out of Todmorden and get off at the Cornholme boundary sign. Otherwise from the end of Frieldhurst Road turn left down the A646 in the direction of Todmorden, keeping to the left hand side of the road. Just before reaching Dundee Road a seat is encountered in an alcove and a bus stop (no. 30) just inside the Cornholme boundary sign. Cross to the bus stop. This is where to get off if you are starting from Section 2. Between the stop and a small green area to the left, planted with half standards, a track leads up the hillside, following a zigzag route which eventually leads to the derelict farmhouse at Roundfield. Hartley Royd can now be seen on the other side of the valley.

Beyond Roundfield, the route continues and, after avoiding a bad area of bog, arrives at another ruined farmhouse. Here a distinct track becomes a gravelly farm road, leading to Wet Shaw, which has just been rebuilt and hugs the hillside in the company of vans and rickety sheds. Continue onwards, following the farm road to New Towneley.

At New Towneley a choice must be made. If you continue onwards, following the track, you will arrive at West End — just beyond which you will be able to follow a descending track which will rejoin the main route above Flail Croft on its way to Todmorden Edge. This short cut will take time and effort off the journey, but will deny you the opportunity of seeing a spectacular bird's eye view of the Upper Calder Gorge and the imposing edifice of Robin Wood Mill, one of the Fieldens' many spinning mills. The Fielden Trail takes the latter option and heads towards the valley. Take the easy option if you like, but I'm going to Robin Wood Mill!

From New Towneley, follow an indistinct route down the pasture towards trees. Orchan Rocks can be seen directly opposite, on the other side of the valley. Halfway down the field the path is soon discovered on the left, running between a fence and a wall. Only trouble is, there's no way of getting to it — when you arrive at the field corner you can see the path leading out onto the crags, but you will

Cornholme to Dawson Weir

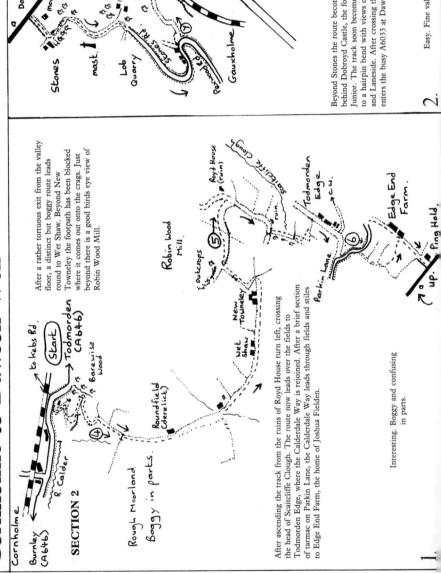

SECTION 2

After a rather tortuous exit from the valley floor, a distinct but boggy route leads round to Wet Shaw. Beyond New Towneley the footpath has been blocked where it comes out onto the crags. Just beyond there is a good birds eye view of Robin Wood Mill.

After ascending the track from the ruins of Royd House turn left, crossing the head of Scaitcliffe Clough. The route now leads over the fields to Todmorden Edge, where the Calderdale Way is rejoined. After a brief section of tarmac on Parkin Lane, the Calderdale Way leads through fields and stiles to Edge End Farm, the home of Joshua Fielden.

Interesting. Boggy and confusing in parts.

SECTION 3

Beyond Stones the route becomes a track which passes behind Dobroyd Castle, the former home of John Fielden Junior. The track soon becomes a metalled road descending to a hairpin bend with views of the Gauxholme Skew Bridge and Laneside. After crossing the Rochdale Canal the route enters the busy A6033 at Dawson Weir.

Easy. Fine valley views.

2.

1.

have to climb over the fence to get to it. Once over the fence, turn right along the edge. Just before the fence meets a wall, coming in from the right, a path may be seen descending the steep slope to the left, marked by a row of stakes. Follow this route down the hillside, and soon another path is met with, ascending from below left. This path comes up from Robin Wood Mill at Lydgate, which can be seen in the valley below.

Robin Wood Mill

This tall, grey edifice, nestling at the bottom of the valley, was once one of the Fieldens' spinning mills. Severely classical in design, it still manages to look imposing, despite broken windows and the fact that much of it now appears to be derelict. What premises are still in use are the premises of The Todmorden Glass Co.

What a handsome building it is. A cotton mill, yes, but quite unlike the Mons Mill further down the valley, which is more typical of a later generation of Lancashire cotton mills, those red brick giants which dominate the landscape around Rochdale, Bury, Oldham and Manchester. Nearby is Fielden View and Robinwood Terrace, a uniform group of houses built in 1864 — to house some of the Fieldens' workers perhaps? Even now, in decay, the community is dominated by the mill and the adjacent railway viaduct.

At this point perhaps we ought to take a look at the cotton industry, which made the Fieldens their fortunes and is therefore closely bound up with the subject of this book. The cotton industry was literally created by self-made men like the Fieldens between the years 1770 and 1840 in a period of spectacular growth. It continued to expand, reaching its peak in 1912 when 8 million yards of cotton were produced. After this date increasing foreign competition along with various other factors were to bring about the gradual decline of the industry. By 1803 cotton had already overtaken wool as Britain's leading export — quite an achievement for an industry based entirely on imported raw materials. The reasons for this sudden boom are varied. The invention of the Saw Gin by Eli Whitney was certainly a contributory factor to cotton's phenomenal growth, for it opened up a supply of cotton from the Southern United States at a time when other sources, for example the West Indies, were beginning to prove inadequate. U.S. growers consistently reduced their prices up to 1898, and this enabled Lancashire to create an industry which was to make the whole world its market.

Why Lancashire? Basically because it had all the right qualifications: cheap land, coal, and soft water which was ideal for bleaching, dyeing and printing, not to mention the powering of machinery. In Liverpool, facing the Americas, 'King Cotton' was to find his port, and in Manchester his market. In Lancashire there were fewer restrictive practices like guilds and ancient corporations to hinder the development of the new industry. In many ways pre-industrial Lancashire was rough, wild and poorly developed, but for the building of a cotton industry conditions were ideal, and, when it came, the growth was simply phenomenal.

The technology which made such a growth possible had been developing for some time. In 1733 the 'Flying Shuttle' devised by John Kay of Bury triggered off a whole pattern of invention which was to transform the whole social and economic structure of those northern regions involved in textile industries. In 1760 came Hargreaves' 'Spinning Jenny', and in the 1770's Arkwright's 'Water Frame'. 1779 saw the invention of Crompton's 'Spinning Mule' and 1785 Cartwright's Power Loom. The development of the steam engine by James Watt ensured the gradual changeover from waterwheels and goits (artificial watercourses) to boilers and mill engines, with subsequent changes in the priorities of mill siting. The demand for coal rather than water and the need for inlets and outlets of raw and finished materials were to bring improved communications in the form of canals, and later, railways. The spate of inventions continued throghout the 19th century: Radcliffe's Dressing Machine (1803) prepared threads for weaving; Dickinson's 'Blackburn Loom' (1828) introduced picking staves; The 'Self Regulating Mule'; 'Ring Spinning'; 'Northrop Looms'; the list goes on, and on, and on.

The production of cotton cloth did not only involve spinning and weaving. The cloth had to be 'finished' and dyed, and a whole series of inventions and processes evolved to improve this area of the industry. Early methods of finishing were costly and slow. This was particularly true of 'bleaching', which in the late 18th century required many acres of grassland for exposing cloth to sunlight and water (crofting). Another process, 'bowking', immersed the cloth in alkaline leys concocted from the ashes of trees and various plants. Cloth was 'soured' in buttermilk and washed in 'becks' filled with running water - all complex and time-consuming processes.

Then came the changes. In 1750 the use of dilute sulphuric acid reduced the time taken for souring by half. In 1785 the French chemist Berthollet devised a chloride of lime bleaching powder. New methods of mass-producing bleacher's materials like soda ash, caustic soda and chlorine gas were also introduced in the 19th century. 1828 saw the introduction of Bentley's 'Washing Machine'; and in 1845 Brook's Sunnyside Print Works in Crawshawbooth used steam power to carry the ropes of cloth through all the stages of the bleaching process. 1860 saw the use of caustic soda by John Mercer of Clayton-le-Moors to produce a silken finish on the cloth, known as 'Mercerisation', and in 1856 Perkins succeeded in extracting mauve aniline dye from coal tar, which up to that time had been a waste product from the gasworks. Previous methods of dyeing had involved up to 19 different processes, including immersion in cow muck!

The impact of all this development upon Lancashire was immense. The whole region was transformed where King Cotton held sway. Cotton brought new mills, machinery, houses, canals and railways. New communities came into being. The development of Todmorden

The Fieldens' spinning mill at Robin Wood, Lydgate.

from a small hamlet into a substantial mill town was almost entirely due to the cotton trade. The mill owner and his operatives were but the tip of the iceberg — a host of interests were involved, from engineers, architects and builders, to chemists, bankers and financiers. Cotton created a demand for textile machinery, steam engines and boilers, houses, gas, electricity and transport. As a result of the cotton boom, Britain's best engineering skills were concentrated in and around Lancashire; and Merseyside's chemical industry owes its origin to cotton's consumption of dyestuffs, bleaching powders and soap. Mining, ironfounding and glassmaking also served the cotton industry. Indeed, it seemed that King Cotton was everyone's employer.

Prosperity and growth however, were not the only new developments at the court of King Cotton. There were other, less agreeable 'innovations' like bad housing and sanitation, grinding poverty, child labour, dangerous working conditions, and, most significantly of all, unbearably long hours. "Overwork," wrote Leon Faucher in 1884, "is a disease which Lancashire has inflicted upon England, and which England in turn has inflicted upon Europe."

It was in this context that the name of Fielden was to become universally esteemed, and to earn a fame far more enduring than that of mere charitable mill magnates, as we shall see. The Fieldens saw the benefits that might be derived from the factory system, but, unlike most of their class, they were painfully aware of the evils it created, and took steps not only towards easing the lot of the working man, but also towards his political emancipation, as we shall soon discover.

The next section of the Fielden Trail leads to Todmorden Edge. After meeting the path coming up from Robin Wood Mill, continue onwards and slightly upwards, contouring round the hillside. Soon there are good views down the valley towards Todmorden, with Centre Vale Park and the Mons spinning mill in the foreground. Mons is a much later mill than Fielden's at Robin Wood, and was built on The Holme, a large open space where fairs and circuses were formerly held. Opposite the remains of Royd House, which is now just a pile of stones overgrown with elder trees, join an ascending track in a gully (passing yet another ruin) which soon arrives at a rusty old gate facing West End on the hillside, to the right of another farm, Dike Green. Here the alternative route from New Towneley is met with. If anybody decided to miss Robin Wood Mill from the itinerary and take the short cut, they will be waiting for you here. Now turn left (you will have to climb over the wooden gate) and follow a green track past the head of Scaitcliffe Clough. At Flail Croft nearby, lived (in 1714)

Samuel Fielden, brother of Nicholas of Edge End, and John of Todmorden Hall, both of whom we will encounter later. Continue onwards until a wall and wooden gate are joined (on left). Pass through this gate, and be careful when you shut it, as when I did so I was miles away in thought and did not see the eye-level barbed wire which made a neat little cut on my forehead! Beyond a stone in the wall on which is carved the letters ⚹ ⋔ bear left across the fields to enter the lane leading to Todmorden Edge.

Todmorden Edge

If Nonconformism had shrines then Todmorden Edge would certainly be one of them, for it has associations with both the early Quakers and the early Methodists. Quaker meetings were held at Todmorden Edge Farm and, as at Shore, there is a 'Quaker Pasture'. Early Quakers were persecuted, and Todmorden Edge has seen its share of that. Henry Crabtree, who was curate of Todmorden in the 1680s, viewed the Friends with great distaste. With Simeon Smith, his servant, he surprised a number of Quakers from Walsden and Todmorden when met together at the house of Daniel Sutcliffe, at Rodhill Hey on May 3rd 1684. A fine of five shillings was imposed on each person present. As the fines were not paid, distraints were made on their goods. A month later, a meeting in Henry Kailey's house at Todmorden Edge was similarly disturbed and goods to the value of £20, an ark of oatmeal, and a pack of wool were taken.

Todmorden must have been noted for the number of Friends, for when those who declined to pay for repairs to the church and school at Rochdale were summoned by the Rochdale Churchwardens, it was stated that the majority of the offenders came from Todmorden, where Quakers were "both numerous and troublesome". Fortunately for the Fieldens and others of their faith 1689 saw the passing of the Toleration Act, which enabled Quakers to register their meeting houses officially for the first time.

In the wake of the Quakers came the Methodists. On 1st May 1747, John Wesley preached at Shore at midday; then later, at Todmorden Edge Farm, he called "a serious people to repent and believe in the Gospel". The following year, on October 18th 1748, the first recorded quarterly meeting ever held in Methodism took place at Chapel House, Todmorden Edge, under the chairmanship of that noted religious firebrand William Grimshaw (who was curate of Todmorden before his more famous association with Haworth). Methodism

Todmorden Edge, looking across the valley to Bridestones.

obtained many converts, and the Friend's Meeting House at Todmorden Edge, along with a Meeting House and a Baptist Chapel at Rodhill End, were sold to the Wesleyans.

The Fieldens, unlike many of their Quaker brethren, were not converted to Methodism. They remained Quakers, but for all that the Methodists were to play an important part in the establishment of Unitarianism in Todmorden, with which the Fieldens were actively involved.

From Todmorden Edge the Fielden Trail moves on to Edge End, the home of Todmorden's first industrial entrepreneur, and father of 'Honest John' Fielden — Joshua Fielden of Edge End. As we leave Todmorden Edge with its Wesleyan associations it is perhaps worth bearing in mind that John Wesley, for all his goodness and unwavering faith, went so far as to recommend child labour as a "means of preventing youthful vice". John Fielden, who was born 36 years later in 1784, would hardly have agreed with such a sentiment.

On meeting the Calderdale Way by the stables at Todmorden Edge Farm, bear right, following the concreted farm road past a white gate to where it meets tarmac at Parkin Lane. From here the route continues without difficulty (following the Calderdale Way) to:-

Edge End Farm

At Edge End we come to an important chapter in the Fielden story. Here is the scene of the Fielden's transition from farming and wool to industry and cotton. This low, embattled stone farmhouse hugging the hillside was where the Industrial Revolution in Todmorden was born. The initiator of the chain of events which was so greatly to transform the fortunes of both the Fieldens and those around them was Joshua Fielden, 'Honest John's' father. Joshua Fielden was not the first of that name, nor would he be the last. His second son was called Joshua, and he was to have a grandson and a great grandson of the same name. As if that was not confusing enough, we also find that his father, grandfather and great grandfather were also called Joshua! Because of this I have found it necessary to number all these 'Joshuas' in the hope of lending at least a little clarity to a confusing and misleading situation.

Back at Hartley Royd we discussed Abraham Fielden of Inchfield who married Elizabeth Fielden of Bottomley in the early 17th century. Their third son, Joshua Fielden of Bottomley, although not the first Fielden to bear that name, was certainly the first Joshua in his line, so for that reason I have referred to him as Joshua (I). From him the Joshua Fieldens of Bottomley and Edge End run as follows:

JOSHUA FIELDEN (I) of Bottomley Quaker. Received Bottomley from brother John of Hartley Royd. Died 1693.

JOSHUA FIELDEN (II) of Bottomley. Died 27th February 1715.

JOSHUA FIELDEN (III) of Edge End. Born Bottomley. Died at Dobroyd. (1701 - 1781)

JOSHUA FIELDEN (IV) of Edge End and later Waterside. (1748 - 1811).

From this we can see that 'Honest John's' father was the fourth successive Joshua in his line. Joshua Fielden (IV) was a Quaker like his forebears, and who lived in "a bleak, pious fashion" at Edge End Farm. His uncle Abraham (1704 - 79) had inherited property at Todmorden Hall (this is a connection we will explore later) and was actively involved in the domestic textile industry. Joshua too, like most of the farmers around him, was involved in the production of woollen cloth, which was the traditional occupation of the whole district. By the mid 18th century the domestic system of cloth production had reached the height of its importance. Originally the farmer/weaver simply produced his cloth at home and carried it to market (a cloth hall had been established as early as 1550 by the Waterhouse family of Shibden). Soon however, the business diversified and expanded: weavers collected into small settlements, the weaving hamlets linked by causeys and packhorse ways; while local merchants often acted as middlemen, selling raw wool to the weavers and buying back the finished cloth. As a result of this, in the 17th and early 18th centuries prosperous clothiers' houses began to appear, many of them with a "takkin' in shop" alongside. By the mid 17th century Halifax had its own cloth hall, but did not completely supersede the Heptonstall one until the Halifax Piece Hall was opened in 1779.

Joshua Fielden, like most farmer/weavers in the Upper Calder Valley, had to work hard for his living. He attended Friends' weekly meetings at Shoebroad, farmed, wove his cloth and every weekend walked to the Halifax market and back with the cloth 'pieces' on his shoulders, a distance of 24 miles. Yet times were changing in the latter years of the 18th century. Maybe Joshua was getting a bad back and sore feet, or perhaps he simply had an eye for the main chance. Whatever his reasons, Fielden realised (in the words of J. T. Ward) that "Todmorden's geography permitted its embryonic industrialists to choose between cotton and wool." It was time to make that choice and Joshua chose cotton, a new material that perhaps offered more exciting prospects than the stolid, traditional pursuits of his forefathers.

Whatever his reasons may have been, Joshua Fielden turned his back on Halifax and was drawn westwards to the markets of Bolton and Manchester. It was time to break away from the established way of things.

In 1782 Joshua Fielden (IV) sold Edge End, packed his bags, bought some spinning jennies and established his cotton business in cottages at Laneside. He could never have realised that in embarking upon this uncertain, risky venture he would be laying the foundations of an industrial empire destined to be one of the largest in the world, and that his children would succeed to a wealth and fame far beyond his wildest imaginings.

From Edge End, continue onwards to the pretty gardens and interesting stone heads of Ping Hold which once had, as its name suggests, a pinfold, where stray animals were kept until they could be claimed from a pinderman on payment of a fine. From here the lane continues onwards, passing the strange, crenellated turrets of the 'model farm' on the Dobroyd Castle Estate, and eventually reaches a

Edge End Farm, home of Joshua Fielden.

large house surrounded by trees, iron railings and a boulder outcrop almost leaning against the windows, which is called (appropriately enough) Stones.

At Stones once lived another Quaker family, the Greenwoods, who were substantial landowners hereabouts. The Stones' Greenwoods originated from Middle Langfield Farm, which was the home of John Greenwood from 1675. In such a closely knit community as this it was inevitable that sooner or later they would find themselves in dynastic alliance with their neighbours, the Fieldens, and so it was that on 4th June 1771 Jenny Greenwood, daughter of James and Sarah Greenwood of Langfield, married Joshua Fielden (IV) of Edge End at the local Friends' Meeting House. The union was fruitful, as she had five sons and four daughters (one of which died in infancy). The third son of her brood was to find lasting fame. He would grow up to become known as 'Honest John' Fielden, humanitarian, Member of Parliament and factory reformer.

Beyond Stones, follow a gradually descending gravelly lane, lined with occasional groups of trees. On the right is a TV mast, and on the left, when the track bears slightly to the right, we are treated to an extremely good view of:-

Dobroyd Castle

Dobroyd Castle is the second of the 'great houses' which were the residences of 'Honest John' Fielden's three sons. Stansfield Hall was, as we have seen, the residence of the youngest son, Joshua Fielden of Stansfield Hall and Nutfield Priory, Surrey. Dobroyd Castle, most certainly the grandest of the three houses, was the residence of the middle son, John Fielden J.P. of Dobroyd Castle and Grimston Park, Leeds.

Dobroyd Castle was built between 1865 and 1869 at a cost of £100,000. When it was completed, 300 of the workmen involved in its construction were treated to a celebration dinner at the Lake Hotel, Hollingworth Lake. Like most of the Fieldens' later buildings, it was designed by John Gibson, who also designed Stansfield Hall.

John Fielden J.P. of Dobroyd Castle was a landowner in the grand style. He was appointed High Sheriff and J.P. in 1844. (However his father had refused to take a justices' oath in protest at the new Poor Law). By 1873 he owned 405 Lancashire acres and 2848 acres in Yorkshire. Ten years later his total rental was £9000. His grandfather Joshua (IV), the 'embryonic industrialist', had taken the Fieldens into the town. Grandson John returned them to the soil once more, but as landed gentry. John Fielden J.P. was the last surviving of 'Honest John's' three sons, dying in July 1893 at the age of 71. He had spent much of his life in a wheelchair as a result of a riding accident which shattered his leg. He was twice married, and in this context is the subject of an interesting story we will encounter further along the Fielden Trail.

Dobroyd Castle was purchased by the Home Office in the 1940's and became an approved school. It is now a community home.

After surveying Dobroyd Castle, continue onwards, following the Calderdale Way down Stones Road, passing a barn and cottage on the left. This is Pex House. Originally called Pighill, it was a substantial farm at one time. It ceased to be when it was sold to John Fielden in 1865, who at that time needed land on which to build his castle. The house was then occupied by Peter Ormerod, father of William Ormerod, the second mayor of Todmorden.

Beyond the barn the descent becomes steeper, and the road soon emerges onto a hairpin bend, perched precipitously on the edge of the

Dobroyd Castle. Residence of John Fielden JP of Grimston Park, 'Honest John' Fielden's son.

valley overlooking Gauxholme. Below, looking almost like a scale model, the canal passes beneath the great skew bridge which carries the railway onto the Gauxholme Viaduct. Here is civilisation at last — mills, terraced houses and the sinews of industry.

At the lodge gate leading to Dobroyd Castle, the metalled road bears sharp right and descends to the Bacup Road at Gauxholme where it meets up with Section 3 of the Fielden Trail (Pexwood Road). Our route however, continues onwards, (sign 'No Through Road'), descending through woodland towards Todmorden as it meanders above the railway. Below, alongside the main road, can be seen the cottages at Laneside in which Joshua (IV) set up his cotton business. Even the railway below us was utilised by the Fieldens' ever expanding industrial empire (they were after all directors of the railway company) — sidings from the Lancashire and Yorkshire Railway were run directly into the two warehouses at Dobroyd, and an overhead gantry carried consignments to and from the mills.

The lane descends to a kissing gate beside the railway line. From here a pedestrian level crossing leads over the tracks. You will notice that the lines are very shiny — that means they are used quite frequently, so please beware of trains!

Having crossed the railway, bear left down to Dobroyd Road. Soon, an old stable block appears on the right, and just beyond it the route passes over the canal to emerge on the busy A6033 Todmorden - Rochdale Road at the side of Dawson Weir, which is the substantial georgian house on the left.

Dawson Weir

At Dawson Weir we stop and reflect awhile, for we have reached yet another chapter in the Fielden story. If you are in need of refreshment to assist this reflection and the hour be right, turn left along the road and treat yourself to fish and chips and pop at the nearby Waterside Chippy — truly scrumptious! Now retrace your steps to Dawson Weir.

On 12th September 1811 'Honest John' Fielden, third son of Joshua (IV) of Edge End and Laneside married Ann Grindrod of Rochdale at Rochdale Parish Church. He was 27 years old, newly married and seeking a home in which to settle down and start a family. The newly-weds set up house here in this fine three-storeyed Georgian house sandwiched neatly between the turnpike and the canal. This was an age when manufacturers still lived close to their workers, and John made a shrewd choice in settling here, right at the heart of the Fielden's expanding industrial empire.

I imagine Dawson Weir as being a happy household, echoing to the patter of children's feet and the murmer of kindly servants. John and Ann were certainly prolific, for in this house were born seven children — three sons and four daughters. The three sons were Samuel (b.1816), John (b.1822) and Joshua (b.1827). The daughters were Jane (b.1814), Mary (b.1817), Ann (b.1819) and Ellen (b.1829). The three boys of course were the 'three brothers', two of which we have already encountered at Stansfield Hall and Dobroyd Castle. Their father was the son of a successful manufacturer who would soon go on to acquire a uniquely individual fame as M.P. for Oldham and a radical reformer — but in these days, although vastly wealthier than many of their neighbours, the Fieldens were nowhere near attaining those trappings of the landed gentry which 'Honest John's' three boys would come to enjoy in later life.

Life at Dawson Weir must have been genteel and moderately comfortable; wealthy by the standards of old Joshua's generation, but

Dawson Weir.

quite bourgeois when set against the princely lifestyles of later Fieldens at Dobroyd Castle, Stansfield Hall and Centre Vale. The house looks rather like a parsonage — early 19th century middle class. A clergyman like Patrick Brontë would certainly have not found Dawson Weir above his station, and indeed the lifestyle of 'Honest John's' family at Dawson Weir must have been very like that which is now observable down to the smallest domestic details in the Bronte Parsonage Museum in Haworth.

But for some personal insights into domestic life there from the pen of John Fielden's second daughter, Mary, there would be little else to say in connection with Dawson Weir. There is nothing sensational in the letters, as they are, for the most part, the letters of a young and rather bossy nineteen year old 'big sister' to her 'kid brother' John at the St. Domingo House School in Liverpool. The letters do however, give insights into daily events in 19th century Todmorden. Here are some examples:

"Dawson Weir

My Dear John,   May 10th 1836.

       You are a very naughty boy not to have written to me since you returned to school . . . I hope after you receive this that you will write and tell me you are alive. I expect my father will be coming here in a little more than a week as the Members of the House [of Commons] have a holiday of about ten days for Whitsuntide. All here are pretty well — you can tell John that Sam has exchanged the old cow for that horse that Sam has heard speak of and John Collinge has been breaking it in, and tell John that John Collinge says he thinks it will soon be ready for ME to ride. It will just do for a ladies' pony. Ask John if he does not think it will look a great deal better with me upon its back than with him.

The weather is so fine at present, it is a delightful change from the bad weather we have had. Sam is so industrious you cannot think — he often gets up at five o' clock in a morning and goes into the mill . . .

Your affectionate sister,

Mary Fielden . . ."

It is not so hard to imagine Mary with her new pony. No doubt her brother's friend had designs on it also, as she seems to be rubbing it in that she had 'bested' him in getting the pony! No doubt she kept it in the old stable block we passed on the other side of the canal.

Not all of Mary's letters brought news so cheerful. Disease and death were constant companions in an age where sickness was rampant, and medical knowledge and hygiene virtually non-existent. In the 1830s the average life expectancy was far lower than it is today. Infant mortality in particular was high, a fact which no doubt explains the tendency of early Victorians to beget large families. The Fielden children at Dawson Weir were luckier than many of their class, for all seven of them managed to grow up and take their place as adults; though their mother, Ann, died in 1831 when Mary was 14 (her youngest sister Ellen was only 2). No doubt she was, like many nineteenth century women, worn out with bearing children.

In 1834 John Fielden took a second wife, Elizabeth Dearden of the 'Haugh' in Halifax. Whether or not Mary liked her new stepmother is unknown, yet by 1836 she was attending yet another funeral, within months of getting her pony:-

	"Dawson Weir
My Dear John,	Sept. 18th 1836.

You will be very surprised and very sorry to hear that we have had another of our friends taken from us — about half past twelve this morning my Aunt Lacy of Stoodley departed this life after an illness of more than a week . . . she had a paralytic stroke which deprived her of the use of her right side . . . We saw my aunt yesterday — she appeared very ill and much altered in appearance since we had seen her the week before. My uncle Lacy is of course very much distressed — but wears the affliction as well as can be expected — Someone will write to you again, either tomorrow or Tuesday and inform you about your mourning."

Betty Lacy (nee Fielden), wife of Henry Lacy of Stoodley Hall, died at Stoodley Hall aged 60. She is buried in the Old Churchyard at Todmorden. The grim theme of sickness and death continues in other letters. Earlier in the same year Mary expressed concern over the condition of her mother, (actually her stepmother, Elizabeth Dearden), who had dropsy in the chest and was seriously ill. (Nowadays this would be diagnosed as severe bronchitis or pneumonia). The prescribed treatment for such a condition seems, to modern eyes, more severe than the condition itself:

"Doctor Henny told her that she required the greatest care, attention and quiet, that she has not to walk much, not to go up and down stairs and not to go uphill. He ordered her a blister and some medicine. She has a blister put on every other morning and lets it remain on for 24 hours when she has it taken off and some healing ointment put on . . . She is at the Haugh and will remain there, I suppose, until she is better. She went last Friday . . . I do not wish you to tell anyone what my mother's complaint is as she might not much like it, and it may be better not . . .

Your attached sister,
Mary Fielden."

A 'blister' or 'blister plaster' was used medically in those days to raise blisters as a counter irritant — it was composed of a compound of Spanish Fly (cantharis), beeswax, resin and lard, to make an externally applied medication. Because of (or more likely despite!) this treatment, Mary's stepmother recovered, to die two years after her husband, in October 1851, at the age of 63.

By this time Mary Fielden had married in the January of the same year, at the age of 34. Her husband was John Morgan Cobbett, son of William Cobbett, the famous radical journalist and author, who was her father's close friend and fellow M.P. John Morgan Cobbett had attended her father's funeral in June 1849, and had no doubt consoled the grieving daughter. Certainly the Fieldens were no strangers to the Cobbetts, for in one of her letters in 1840 Mary states that "Mr. James and Mr. Richard Cobbett came here on Saturday night — Mr. Richard went back to Manchester this morning, but Mr. James is still here . . ." These were presumably John Morgan Cobbett's brothers. Perhaps Mary's husband-to-be was the John who was at school with her brother, the one she 'bested' over the pony. Who knows? Whatever the case may have been, they were certainly well-acquainted.

After her wedding Mary left Todmorden and went to live with her husband at Farnham, Surrey (where there is now a Cobbett Museum). She bore him two sons, John Fielden Cobbett and William Cobbett and a daughter, Mary. Her husband died in 1877 and is buried at Farnham.

We will leave Mary Fielden with an amusing but also sadly revealing anecdote. As Ian Dewhirst has pointed out in his History of Keighley, emigration caused by hardship, poverty and the threat of the workhouse was a common phenomenon in the 1840s and '50s. Even the penniless could escape abroad for a consideration; it was so easy, in fact, that men would often ship out for California or the Cape of Good Hope, abandoning wife and children to the workhouse:

"Dawson Weir. March 23rd 1840.

to John Fielden M.P.
17 Panton Square
Westminster.

My Dear Father, . . . have you heard that William Greenwood the grocer (who came to chapel) went along with Thomas Dawson to America. It is said that he is gone out of the way of his creditors because he is in debt — but I have heard that they can pay their debts, if they receive what is owing to them. He has left his wife and family behind, and is gone intending to buy a piece of land, and if he thinks he can do well he will either send for or fetch his family . . ."

We can only speculate as to whether or not he ever did. Perhaps there is someone now living in some part of the United States who can supply the answer?

We have now reached the end of Section 2. If you parked your car at the start of Section 1, you will find it just five minutes walk away. Simply turn left for Todmorden Town Centre. If, however, your car is at the beginning of Section 2, you will have to follow the Burnley Road all the way up to Cornholme (catch the Burnley bus.)

SECTION 3

Rake End via Gauxholme, Inchfield, Walsden and Bottomley

Now if you wish to continue or are starting Section 3, follow the road right from Dawson Weir towards Walsden. Just beyond Dobroyd Court, still on the right, you will pass some firemen's houses, with a beautifully carved Todmorden coat-of-arms over the front door. Opposite, on the other side of the road, is Waterside Mills, once the Fieldens' chief seat of manufacture, which will be discussed elsewhere. Beyond a mill gate and a clock on the right, Waterside House and the Laneside cottages appear on the left, opposite a council yard. This is the start of Section 3 of the Fielden Trail.

Laneside

Here, facing heaps of road grit in a council yard across the busy main road, stand the original cottages where Joshua Fielden (IV) set up his cotton business in 1782, after moving down here from Edge End. As a yeoman farmer, he had, with two or three handlooms at his disposal, combined farming with cloth manufacture at Edge End. Now, at Laneside he abandoned woollen manufacture and became a cotton spinner. The cottages you see here originally had two storeys. When Joshua Fielden moved here his family occupied one of the cottages, the other two being used for spinning. By this time he had been married nearly eleven years and had fathered two sons, Samuel and Joshua; and three daughters, Mary, Betty and Salley. (Mary Fielden of Dawson Weir was their niece — Betty Fielden being the 'Aunt Lacy' referred to in Mary's letter).

At Laneside the family prospered, mainly as a result of caution and hard work. They managed to keep consistently employed and gradually expanded their business as trade increased. A third storey was added, along with a warehouse crane (the walled-up hole where it was mounted is still visible in the centre of the building). Later, when they decided to use steam power, they built a stone mill of five storeys

Dawson Weir to Bottomley

THE ROCHDALE CANAL

Surveyed by James Brindley in 1765 then put into the hands of John Rennie, who was asked to design and build it. In 1793 it was re-surveyed by William Jessop, who was finally responsible for building the canal. (1794-1802).

1.

Uncomplicated. But potentially confusing.

Dawson Weir

ROCHDALE CANAL   A 6033   Todmorden

Littleboro

Start   Waterside
SECTION 3

Laneside.
(Birthplace of 'Honest John' Fielden.)

Follow road from Laneside. At Bar Street turn left onto canal towpath, and follow towpath under Skew Bridge to Bacup Road at Gauxholme.

to Slones →

Pexwood Road   GAUXHOLME.

to Bacup (A681)

UP.R.   Naze (ruin).

Law Hey.

Just beyond Pexwood Road turn left onto Naze Road. Beyond tripe factory, follow winding track up hillside to the ruin at Naze. Fine views across valley to the Basin Stone and Gaddings. Beyond Naze, track runs between walls and eventually joins track which bears left to Pasture Side.

2.

Rough Hey Lane.

Lumbutts →

Todmorden →

ACROSS L.

P.O.

A6033   Rodd.
Chapel

Inchfield Fold.

WALSDEN.

Calf Hey

Fir Wood

Knowsley Wood

Nickley

Heys

Pasture Side

Down L.

Foul Clough Road

Beyond Pasture Side turn left and follow Rough Hey Lane down the hillside. At the edge of the wood bear right and follow along edge to Nickley (once owned by Fieldens). Follow road down to Walsden.

3.

St Peter's WALSDEN.

ACROSS

Travis Mill Lock

Birks Wood.

mast.

Winterbutlee Lock

Bankwood Bridge.

SLONES

4.

Shaw-LEE   Lightbank   Bottomley.

Dean Royd

Deanroyd Br.

Sands Lock

Bottomley Bridge.

Summit Tunnel

and seven windows in length alongside one of the cottages (this is now demolished). The family home was also improved upon, the more grandly styled Waterside House being built onto the southern end of the cottages.

Four more children were born to the family at Laneside. Three sons, John, James and Thomas, and another daughter Ann (who died in infancy), raising the family total to nine. Here is the complete list with dates:

Samuel (1772-1822)
Mary (1774-1812)
Betty (1776-1836)
Joshua (1778-1847)
Salley (1780-1859)
John ('Honest John') (1784-1849)
Ann (1786-1786)
James (1788-1852)
Thomas (1790-1869)

Life at Laneside must have been rather more spartan than that of succeeding generations. After all, there was a business to be established and a living to be made and, as was usually the case in the Lancashire cotton industry, you weren't spared the long hours and the hard work merely because you happened to be "t' maister's lad"!

John Fielden and his brothers were brought up "to the mill." From the age of 10 John worked 10 hours daily in the mill. Every Tuesday he would set off from Todmorden at 4am with his father to sell cloth in Manchester, returning around midnight with a cart full of raw cotton, having walked a distance of around 40 miles. It was a hard life and no doubt helped to form the attitudes and opinions that would be displayed by 'Honest John' in later life, when he was an M.P. fighting for the rights of his workers. His brothers also were to develop similarly radical opinions.

Why the sons of an old Tory like Joshua Fielden should grow up to become uncompromising radicals no doubt perplexed the pious old man. The boys appeared to Joshua to be "as arrant Jacobins as any in the kingdom." No doubt their education was a contributory factor. These were not the days when the sons of manufacturers were sent to private boarding schools for the wealthy; on the contrary, they were lucky to get an education at all. John and his brother were educated by a village school-master who could neither read nor write but yet turned out pupils who were excellent readers and writers. This schoolmaster was well known for his Jacobin views: he supported the aims and ideals of the French Revolutionaries and instilled these ideas into his pupils. Not surprisingly, when political feeling was running high at the end of the 18th century, Joshua, the strong Tory, decided to remove his sons from the influence of "the holder of such revolutionary opinions". He obviously did so, but one suspects that perhaps it was rather like shutting the stable door after the horse had bolted!

Joshua retired in 1803 though he lived on until 1811. The eldest brothers, Sam, Joshua and John took over management of the business, and changed the name of the firm to Fielden Brothers; while at some time after the death of Samuel in 1822, the premises became known as Waterside. Year by year the business expanded, first hand spinning, then water frames, then steam. In 1829 a large weaving shed

The cottages at Laneside, the birthplace of 'Honest John' Fielden. His father Joshua Fielden began cotton spinning in these cottages after moving from Edge End in 1782, and the little gable that carried the hoist for the cotton is clearly visible.

with a capacity for 800 looms was erected. At the time of its construction it was the biggest shed in the world. More spinning mills were built, and a second, even bigger weaving shed was erected. By 1844 the Fieldens had their own private railway siding and warehouses. Individual members of the family bought smaller mills from time to time, all used for spinning, in the valleys which ran up into the hills from the main valley. They owned mills as far afield as Mytholmroyd, and whole communities — Lumbutts for example — depended entirely on the Fieldens for their livelihood.

In the early days at Laneside the consumption of cotton was small, little more than a weekly cartload. But as transport improved so did the amount of cotton which could be processed in the Fielden's mills. In 1846 some 400 bales were used each week, each containing 500 lbs. In 1830 gasworks were constructed to light the mills — this being the first gasworks to be established by any private concern.

Even at the tender age of seventeen John Fielden began to show an interest in the welfare of his workers. In 1803 he and his brother Joshua opened a Sunday School in a large room where they taught reading, writing and arithmetic to the children who were employed in the factories during the week, and for whom there were no other chances for education. When in 1806 the town proposed forming a Sunday School Union for raising funds for the education of the children of the district's poor, John was one of the workers in the movement, and, for at least 12 years taught and superintended in the three voluntary schools of the Union, where 700 children were taught every Sunday, who (says the 1818 report) "were it not for the institution would remain in the grossest ignorance and spend the sabbath in a very unbecoming manner." The annual cost of educating these 700 schoolchildren was less than £60. Later Fielden was to run a school of his own for the town children, and this developed as a result of the birth of a new force in the religious affairs of the area: Unitarianism.

By 1817 Fielden Bros. employed 3000 handloom weavers. Wages did not exceed 10 shillings a week and when power looms came on the scene they fell as low as three and four shillings. Children at this time often learnt at home to weave, the warp and weft being brought to outlying farmsteads from spinning mills in the valley. Weavers with two ordinary looms received eight shillings a week; a loom with sheeting, 12 shillings. Loom Tacklers were much better paid, receiving 18 to 20 shillings a week. No doubt they enjoyed other privileges too — a verse in the old song "Poverty Knock" runs:

"Tuner should tackle me loom
he'd rather sit on his bum
he's far too busy a courtin' our Lizzie
an' ah cannot get him ta coom . . ."

The days of the handloom weavers however, were numbered. Progressively the Fieldens moved away from manual methods in step with the rest of the expanding cotton industry, and turned to factories and power looms. Such a process could not be halted — it was inevitable. They had to keep up with the times. In 1829 Laneside and Waterside were merged, and, as we have already mentioned, a giant weaving shed was built. The Fieldens nevertheless actively aided the declining handloom weavers.

By the 1830's poverty and unemployment were widespread. The average weekly wage of the inhabitants in outlying districts in 1833 was 4s 3d, or 10s 3d per family. Corn was expensive, and oatmeal, skimmed milk and hard cheese formed the main diet of the working classes. For those without a job the predicament was even worse. The bad situation in the industrial north was by no means helped when in 1834 the Poor Law Amendment Act was passed, which forced the unemployed to accept hard labour and imprisonment and humiliation in the workhouse. The Fieldens' active (and at one point violent) opposition to the new Poor Law forestalled the establishment of a Union Workhouse in Todmorden for many years, and forced the guardians to give outdoor relief.

After the Napoleonic Wars, fierce post-war competition had forced Fieldens to increase their working hours from 10 to 12 (11 on Saturdays). Horrific as this sounds, it was, nevertheless, fewer hours than those worked in most cotton mills at that time. To feel obliged to lengthen the hours of labour at a time when technological changes were making conditions more unpleasant shamed the radical mill masters and brought them out in support of factory reform. John Fielden was especially moved at the plight of the handloom weavers. In 1835 he wrote that he was "applied to by scores of handloom weavers who were so pressed down in their conditions as to be obliged to seek such work, and it gave me and my partners no small pain to be compelled to refuse work to the many that applied for it."

What was life like, then, in the new factories? In Todmorden, the Fieldens' mills and sheds stretched from Laneside to the heart of Todmorden, creating a solid block of industrial buildings that exists to this day. In 1835 they entered the merchant's house of Wildes

Pickersgill in Liverpool and eventually owned warehouse premises as well as properties in Manchester. Even though the Fieldens were the most enlightened of mill masters, actively concerned with the welfare of their operatives, conditions in mills were, nevertheless, harsh by modern standards. During the agitation for Factory Reform numerous books and pamphlets were published, some whitewashing the industry and describing conditions as ideal, others portraying cotton mills as "hell on earth". What were the facts?

One thing is certain: cotton mills were usually dirty, ill-ventilated and filled with unguarded machinery. Dust was often a problem. The air was filled with minute particles of cotton called 'Fly'. The worst place for this was the 'Scutching Room' where bales of cotton were opened and prepared for the machines. In a Scutching Room the dust was often so dense that it enshrouded the workers like a fog. Temperatures could also be most uncomfortable. In a weaving shed it could get as hot as 92 deg. F. Ventilation varied from mill to mill, sometimes good, sometimes bad. Often it was the fault of the operatives themselves: underfed, badly clothed, they had a dread of cold air and would not open the windows. There were no safety regulations and moving parts were not screened or guarded. Driving belts with adjustable buckles were particularly dangerous. The shaft which delivered the power from the mill engine ran along under the ceiling and had drums on it at intervals, connected to the machines by drive belts. A careless mill girl could get her clothes (or worse still her hair) caught in the buckle on the moving belt and be flung over the driving shaft. There was no compensation for accidents, and families of victims had to rely on the charity of their workmates or the mill master.

Work was tedious and tiring. Mule spinning for example entailed walking endlessly to and fro. In 1832 John Fielden was elected first ever M.P. for Oldham. (This was a new seat created by the Reform Bill). One day, he and some fellow M.P.s met a deputation of working people in Manchester, one of whose delegates gave him a statement which contained a calculation of the number of miles which a child had to walk in a day in minding the spinning machine. It amounted to 25 miles! Adding the distance to and from home each day, the distance was often pushed up to 30 miles. 'Honest John' was naturally surprised at this revelation and wasted no time in investigating his own mills. To his dismay, he found that children there were walking nearly as far.

Last of all there were the hours. In his book The Curse of The Factory System, John Fielden laid the blame for all of the ills of the cotton industry at this single door. To reduce the monotony, to improve the health and safety of the workers, to prevent children from falling asleep at machines and walking these fantastic distances it was necessary to do one single thing - reduce the appalling hours of work.

However good the mills were, the hours were apt to vary enormously. Cotton was ruled by the trade cycle. If trade was bad there could be months of enforced idleness with short time and unemployment. When trade was good there was terrible overwork. It was by no means unknown to begin work at 6 am on Monday and work through till 11 at night on the following Tuesday. Then you would start at 6 am again on Wednesday and work through until 11pm on Thursday. Then you would finally start on Friday at 6 am and work until 8pm Saturday. Sunday was the Lord's Day. You got up early and went to worship. With these working times the total working week added up to around 120 hours. It is hardly surprising that accidents were so frequent with workers dozing off and falling into the machinery.

'Honest John' Fielden realised that such hours as these were not merely unjust, they were criminal — "a curse". Consequently he dedicated his life toward attaining a Ten Hours Bill, arguing, rightly as it turned out, that short time would not serve to reduce efficiency and output, but would actually increase it. In pursuit of this aim he was single-minded and uncompromising. Yet John Fielden went further. Unlike many factory reformers, Fielden held Chartist principles and argued that the workers had a right not only to fairer working conditions, but also to an education and political emancipation. He was a true champion of the working man, and we will discuss his political career further along the Fielden Trail.

Back onto the Fielden Trail: from Laneside continue onwards along the road, towards Gauxholme, to reach Bar Street, where there is access to the canal towpath. Turn left here, passing a lock. Restoration work is in progress at time of writing — already the canal has been made navigable between Hebden Bridge and Todmorden, and work gangs are expanding outwards at both ends. It is sad that the canal was allowed to get into such a poor condition in the first place. Only now are we becoming aware of the immense amenity value of our inland waterways, but whether or not any 'real' jobs will emerge from this highly commendable restoration project yet remains to be seen. One can only hope that some lasting good will come out of it.

But back to the Fielden Trail. After passing Shade Lock the towpath runs under the railway beneath a superbly constructed skew bridge. The railway passes over here at a height of about 40 feet as it runs along the Gauxholme Viaduct. This section of railway, Hebden Bridge to Summit, was opened on 31st December 1840, the first passenger service along it being in March 1841. The Gauxholme Viaduct has 17 stone spans of 35 feet. This skew bridge over the canal has a 101 foot span with stone turrets at either end. It represents a considerable feat of engineering for its time. The girders are inscribed "R.J. Butler Stanningley Leeds 1840".

After passing Gauxholme Lowest Lock, immediately beneath the skew bridge, the towpath continues onwards towards Gauxholme. Pexwood Road can now be seen descending on the right, almost parallel with the canal. The next lock, Gauxholme Middle, is a place to reflect awhile before leaving the canal in favour of the neighbouring hills.

As might be expected, the story of the Fieldens is closely tied up with the arrival of both the canal and the railway. We have already seen how the Fieldens used the railway to their private advantage. Their enthusiasm for it, and the trading benefits it brought, had always been immense. It comes as a bit of a surprise therefore, to discover that when some 50 years earlier in 1790, a group of businessmen met in Hebden Bridge to propose a canal from Sowerby Bridge to Manchester, the Fieldens of Laneside were among the group of local mill owners who opposed the scheme!

The reason for this opposition was water. The canal promoters planned to divert streams feeding the river to supply the navigation, thus reducing the need to build numerous catchment reservoirs of their own. The Fieldens, along with most of the other Calderdale mill masters, insisted that they needed all of the available water for their mill goits in order to power machinery and to facilitate their bleaching, dyeing, fulling and printing processes. They complained that, in times of drought, mills would sustain considerable financial losses for want of water, and that the expanding industry, which was creating new mills in large numbers, was further stretching the already limited water resources. Water was all-important to the mill masters, as it was often used again and again, falling from mills high up in the moors to newer mills in the valley bottoms. Indeed water was vital to their livelihood.

Because of this, when the Rochdale Canal Bill came before Parliament, it was thrown out on its second reading because of petitioning by mill owners and the proposals of a rival canal company which suggested a "less troublesome" route down the Ryburn Valley, which would have involved a tunnel under Blackstone Edge. In 1792 the Rochdale promoters held another meeting and resolved to try again. This time they set out to appease the mill owners, whose opposition they had previously underestimated.

It was suggested that only excess water should be fed into the canal, and under normal conditions streamways would flow under the canal, following their normal course. This time opposition softened slightly, so much so that a group of Todmorden mill owners were actually converted to supporting the canal. Among them were the Fieldens, who began to realise that the benefits of a canal might come to outweigh the disadvantages. The battle continued, but eventually, after agreeing to build catchment reservoirs on the moors, which would supply both mills and canals, the Rochdale promoters began to see light. Times were changing — steam engines were being installed in the mills, and it was apparent that the manufacturer's needs would soon be for coal rather than for water. On 4th April 1794 the Rochdale Canal Act was finally passed by Parliament.

Work began immediately, although the canal was not completed until 1802. The Act of Parliament for the Rochdale Canal gives a list of streams where only surplus water was available for the canal company. The streams were almost all in the Todmorden area, and many of them had Fielden properties along their courses — Mitgelden Clough, Warland Clough, Stoodley Clough and Lumbutts Stream. One entry reads:

"At the call or weir next above Todmorden belonging to Joshua Fielden", water might be turned into the canal "only when the stream shall flow over such call or weir more than 2 7/12 inches mean depth and 30 feet broad . . ."

By August 1798 the navigation was completed as far as Todmorden, and barges were bringing in coal and raw cotton. The canal company at the outset charged 2d per mile per ton of merchandise when a lock was passed, otherwise 1½d per mile. Fielden Bros., one of the first companies to go over to steam power, profited immensely from the new navigation, yet water still continued to be a problem (especially after the Manchester section was opened) and it wasn't until 1827 that the canal finally had an adequate water supply (by which time we are on the eve of 'The Railway Age').

Nevertheless the Rochdale Canal played its part: barges brought in raw cotton and took away calicoes, fustians and velveteens. At this time 60,000 lbs of cotton were being spun weekly in Todmorden, and 7000 pieces of calico manufactured, so the Fielden's consumption of cotton had gone way beyond old Joshua's weekly horse and cart.

In 1825 a company was formed with the intention of building a Manchester to Leeds Railway, and in 1830 George Stephenson and

James Walker surveyed a route that would largely follow the line of the Rochdale Canal. The canal company, naturally enough, offered fierce resistance, but its days were numbered. Ironically the same 'progress' that had created the canal now brought about its demise.

Today the days of commercial carrying on the Rochdale Canal are long past, as MSC funded schemes struggle to develop it into an 'amenity waterway'. At present, the section of the canal that has been made navigable does not link up with the other navigable waterways and the Rochdale remains cut off from the rest of the northern canal network. We can only hope that all the ambitious plans of the restorers do not come to nought.

Continuing on our way, the towpath soon passes under the A681 Bacup Road, to arrive at Gauxholme Highest Lock, which has a massive set of new lock gates, the whole lock having been magnificently restored. Now it is time to leave the canal (for the moment at any rate), and to climb out of the valley. Turn right, passing over the lock footbridge. Opposite, a little further along the canal, is the Navigation Supply Co. which is housed in canalside buildings where there was once stabling for 14 boat horses and 14 cart horses, this being the old Gauxholme Wharf. Having crossed the bridge over the lock, bear right, passing through a gateway onto the Bacup Road. Opposite is the bottom of Pexwood Road which leads up the hillside to Dobroyd Castle and Stones. Not too long ago the hillside here was wooded, and somewhere near this road junction on Friday April 25th 1755 a crowd gathered at the bottom of Pexwood to hear the preaching of John Wesley. The relevant entry in Wesley's diary reads as follows:

"About ten I preached near Todmorden. The people stood row above row on the side of the mountain. They were rough enough in outward appearance, but their hearts were as melting wax. One can hardly conceive anything more delightful than the vale from which we rode from thence; the river ran through the green meadows on the right and the fruitful hills and woods rose on either hand . . ."

Shortly afterwards Wesley also preached and stayed at nearby General Wood, where he had a shirt repaired.

Here at Gauxholme, the Edge End Fieldens had a mill. From the will of Nicholas Fielden of Edge End, 1714:

"Item, I give and devise unto my said son Nicholas fourscore and ten pounds, together with all my right, title, benefit, etc. . . . and unto all that one drying killn, watercorn milln, and raising milln, commonley called Gauxholme Milln, and with the appurtenances, when he shall attaine ye age of twenty and four years . . . I witness whereof I, the said Nicholas ffeilden have hereunto put my hand and seal the ninth day of November 1714 . . .

Nicholas ffeilden of Edge End in Hundersfield in the County of Lancaster, Clothier."

Having entered the Bacup Road from the canal, turn left, and follow the route carefully to the gully behind Law Hey Farm, which is now derelict. Soon the left hand fence gives way to a low bank of earth and stone, more reminiscent of Cornwall — where such dikes take the place of stone walls — than Yorkshire. At the end of this bank we arrive at the ruins of Naze — a pile of rubble and dark stones in the midst of which stands an incongruous modern brick arched fireplace. Here are good views over to Stones.

From Naze the route leads without undue difficulty to Pasture Side. Just beyond Pasture Side turn left onto Rough Hey Lane, and follow it down the hillside to emerge on the edge of the valley overlooking Walsden, above woodland. Turn right, following the wall to Foul Clough Road opposite a three storeyed dwelling (Nicklety). This was once owned by Fieldens. Turn left, following the road steeply downhill to Inchfield Fold.

Inchfield

Inchfield has very long established associations with the Fieldens, although one would hardly realise this, looking at the present buildings. Here lived the Nicholas Fielden who we encountered in Section 1 courting Christobel Stansfield. Here also lived his son, Abraham, who married Elizabeth, the daughter and co-heiress of James Fielden of Bottomley, thus uniting two branches of Fieldens.

By the early 17th century the Inchfield Fieldens were starting to proliferate and prosper. Abraham's brothers were firmly established at Shore, Hartley Royd and Mercerfield. Now, stemming from this new marriage, succeeding generations of Fieldens were to become associated with Bottomley, which is the next stopping point on our journey. Abraham was not the last Fielden to be associated with Inchfield. On the authority of the farmer's wife at Inchfield Fold I am informed that the three storeyed house at Nicklety belonged to one Thomas Fielden; and that the nearby mill, Inchfield Foundry, belonged to one Josiah Fielden, whose sister lived nearby at Inchfield House. Inchfield Fold Farm bears a datestone with the initials GTM 1631 and these, I am told, are the initials of George Travis, who built the house. What of the Fieldens? Well, according to 'Honest John's' family tree there are no 'Fieldens of Inchfield' mentioned after the early 17th century, so perhaps the land was sold off to George Travis, who built the present house.

From Inchfield Fold we simply follow the road into Walsden, emerging onto the busy A6033 road near the local branch library on the left. Cross the road to the Post Office opposite. Here is a chance to purchase refreshments if required.

Walsden is one of those place names with Celtic associations. Like Walshaw near Hebden Bridge it contains the place name element 'Walsh' or 'Welsh' — the English term for 'foreigner', implying that there was a 'British' (ie Celtic) enclave in this area for many centuries after the English (and probably also Norman) conquests. Only the English could come along and call the native British 'foreigners' in their own country!

From Walsden Post Office continue onwards towards the church, and on reaching the canal bridge turn right onto the towpath, passing Travis Mill Lock on the left. From here onwards, until we reach Bottomley Bridge we simply follow the canal towpath again.

The Rochdale Canal on this section of the walk is now newly restored. It is a haunt for anglers and waterfowl, and the views to crags and steep hillsides are fascinating. The Rochdale Canal is soon joined by the railway on the right, which, just beyond Bottomley Bridge enters the Summit Tunnel, the first airshaft of which can be seen up on the hillside.

Before we set off for Bottomley let me give you some bits of information about this magnificent railway tunnel, which, when it was constructed, was regarded as being the wonder of its age. Work began on its construction in the spring of 1838, and on 5th September 1839 it claimed the lives of three men and two boys. On 22nd January 1840 three more workers were killed in the tunnel. By 31st March of that year the cost of the tunnel had exeeded the original estimate by £47,051. Finally, on 11th December 1840 the last brick was keyed in with a silver trowel. According to an account in the Manchester Guardian: "Gentlemen of the first respectability accompanied by numbers of ladies were seen with lighted candles advancing toward the place to witness the ceremony of the completion of the great work. The ladies and gentlemen present were invited to a cold collation at the Summit Inn, while the workmen were regaled within the tunnel". At the time of its completion the Summit Tunnel was the longest railway tunnel in the world, 2885 yards long and containing 23 million bricks.

At Bottomley Bridge we turn left, passing bungalows to ascend a superbly paved packhorse track which snakes up the hillside to Bottomley.

Bottomley

Bottomley is a key place in our Fielden saga. Generations of Quaker (and earlier) Fieldens lived and worked here, and at one time this small cluster of buildings was a small weaving settlement of some note, being situated on the Salter Rake Gate, the main packhorse route over to Lumbutts and Mankinholes, which was an eastern branch of the better known Reddyshore Scout Gate. (The word 'gate' in this context means 'way', and is an old Scandinavian word.) Cotton was spun in later times at nearby Waterstalls Mill. At Bottomley in 1561 lived James Fielden, son of another (unknown) Fielden who lived here in the reign of Edward VI. This James Fielden was great grandfather to the Elizabeth Fielden who married Abraham Fielden of Inchfield. The line runs as follows:

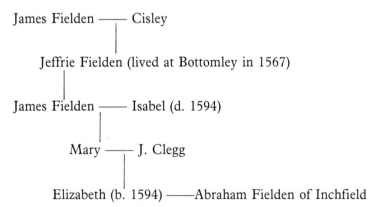

James Fielden ——— Cisley

Jeffrie Fielden (lived at Bottomley in 1567)

James Fielden ——— Isabel (d. 1594)

Mary ——— J. Clegg

Elizabeth (b. 1594) ———Abraham Fielden of Inchfield

Abraham and Elizabeth's sons, John and Joshua, as we have already mentioned became Quakers, and from them all the 'Bottomley Fieldens' are descended.

When I arrived at Bottomley whilst surveying the Fielden Trail, the weather was stifingly hot and the farmer there, Mr. Stansfield, invited us (the dog and I) in for a drink. Mr. Stansfield told me that as a boy he had farmed up at Kebs and Bridestones (this is, of course Stansfield ancestral territory). I thought it strange that just as Nicholas Fielden had inherited Stansfield lands by marriage way back in the 16th century, now, in the 20th century a Stansfield was in possession of lands that had traditionally belonged to the Fieldens since time immemorial! Strange indeed are the workings of fate.

Before we continue on our way, here is a little anecdote concerning the Fieldens of Bottomley:

"When Jane Fielden was a girl of nine years old, her grandfather, Samuel Fielden of Bottomley gave her a soup plate, which bears on the flat part a florid picture of Katharine of Aragon, stating that it belonged to her great grandmother and grandmother, who was then dead. 'It had always belonged to a Jane . . .' She kept it carefully until as an old widow woman living with her daughter at Strines Barn Walsden, she gave it to her grand daughter Jane Crowther, afterwards

Bottomley, home of the Quaker Fieldens.

wife of John Travis, who gave it, (again) to her niece Jane (Crossley) Stenhouse, a few years before her death; so that the piece of old delfware is still travelling with the name 'Jane' . . .

From Bottomley the route crosses Bottomley Clough to emerge behind Deanroyd Farm. Then an old packhorse route, paved in parts, contours along the hillside to Hollingworth Gate, where we enter a metalled road leading to North Hollingworth.

Hollingworth too, has Fielden associations: Abraham and Elizabeth Fielden's son, Joshua (1) of Bottomley ('Honest John's' great-great grandfather) married Martha Greenwood of Hollingworth before a J.P. on 21st October 1656. Their third son, Thomas, inherited Hollingworth, and he lived there until his death in 1762. There are three farmsteads here: Hollingworth Gate, South Hollingworth and North Hollingworth. As to which of these three houses was the residence of Thomas Fielden, is a question I am unable to answer. I would hazard a guess at South Hollingworth, but really the 'Fieldens of Hollingworth' demand more intensive research.

From Hollingworth Gate the tarmac road continues to North Hollingworth. Here, turn right, then left to a walled lane leading to a gate at the edge of open moorland. Beyond the gate is an extremely well preserved packhorse causey, which leads over moorland to Rake End. This is the Salter Rake Gate, an ancient route dating back to times unrecorded.

For my money this is one of the most interesting parts of the Fielden Trail. True, we have encountered old packhorse ways before, most notably at West Whirlaw, but in my view this is one of the most dramatic (and least chronicled) sections of packhorse track in the district. As its name suggests, salt was carried along this route from the salt pans (or 'Wiches') of Cheshire; yet all manner of goods and chattels, not to mention people, must have passed this way down through the centuries (until the Industrial Revolution that is!). Today, there is just the occasional rambler and the moorland wind and rain. What is most striking about this ancient moorland route is its sheer narrowness. If one packhorse train were to meet another coming from the opposite direction there is no way they would have been able to pass each other without one train or the other having to give way and take to the moor. No doubt the issue as to who should 'Give Way' created many a heated argument long ago, when these lonely moorland tracks were busy arteries of communication.

The old causey ascends the hillside to Rake End, where it meanders round the moor edge at the point where the Walsden Valley gives way to Calderdale. A faint path soon appears on the right, heading up the open moor towards the Basin Stone and Gaddings Reservoir. Here is the end of Section 3. For those wishing to get off the Fielden Trail at this point, simply follow the old packhorse way onwards to the Shepherd's Rest Inn on the Lumbutts Road. From here, turn left along the road, then after about a quarter of a mile, turn right down the farm road which eventually leads to Fielden Square in Todmorden (following the Calderdale Way), passing Shoebroad and picking up the latter part of Section 4 en route.

SECTION 4

Todmorden via Basin Stone, Withens Gate, Stoodley Pike, Mankinholes and Lumbutts.

Now at last we come to the final (and wildest) section of the Fielden Trail. The going from here on gets tougher, the route becoming a high level traverse along the edge of the watershed from Gaddings to Stoodley Pike Monument, via Withens Gate. If the weather is awful and you are badly equipped and/or tired then this is the time to think about that nice cosy car parked down in Todmorden. Remember it's not too late (yet!). If however you have walked all the way from Stansfield Hall and have set your heart on doing 'the whole thing' — well, let's get going then! If on the other hand you are starting Section 4 'fresh', here are the directions to get to it — from Fielden Square follow the Calderdale Way past Shoebroad, then follow the track up to Lumbutts Road. Turn left to the Shepherd's Rest. Go through the gate opposite and bear right to the walled lane heading up the moor. This leads directly to Rake End, which is on the edge of the moor, along the causey.

After leaving Salter Rake Gate follow the path up the moorside to the Basin Stone, which is quite unmistakable.

The Basin Stone

A giant stone mushroom, the Basin Stone affords an excellent view over the Walsden Valley. Nicklety and Inchfield, encountered earlier, may be seen across the valley. This bizarre rock formation is the result of natural erosion, centuries of scouring by wind and rain. The Basin Stone looks almost like a pulpit, and it is perhaps not surprising therefore to discover that it has, on occasion, served exactly that purpose. Wesley is reputed to have preached here, and although I have found no evidence to give truth to this story, I would not be in the least bit surprised to discover that he had. Wesley certainly had a penchant for moorland crags as his initials carved on rocks at Widdop testify.

Hollingworth Gate to Withens Gate

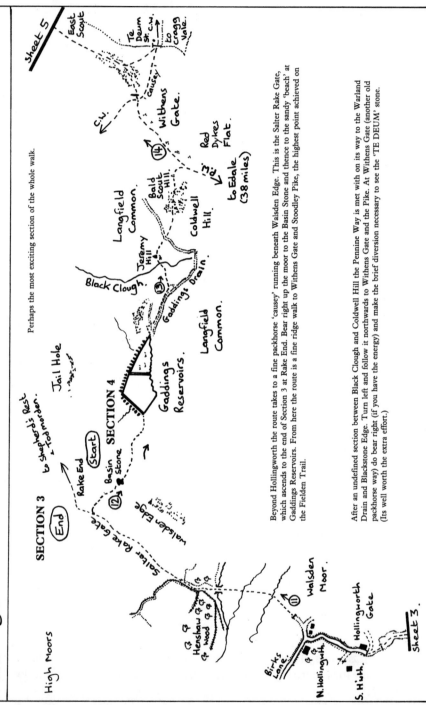

Perhaps the most exciting section of the whole walk.

Beyond Hollingworth the route takes to a fine packhorse 'causey' running beneath Walsden Edge, which ascends to the end of Section 3 at Rake End. Bear right up the moor to the Basin Stone and thence to the sandy 'beach' at Gaddings Reservoirs. From here the route is a fine ridge walk to Withens Gate and Stoodley Pike, the highest point achieved on the Fielden Trail.

After an undefined section between Black Clough and Coldwell Hill the Pennine Way is met with on its way to the Warland Drain and Blackstone Edge. Turn left and follow it northwards to Withens Gate and the Pike. At Withens Gate (another old packhorse way) do bear right (if you have the energy) and make the brief diversion necessary to see the 'TE DEUM' stone. (Its well worth the extra effort.)

Evangelism was not the only force to beckon crowds of people to these remote moorland fastnesses. There were other, more secular causes to be fought for. The year 1842 saw considerable industrial and political unrest. In the summer of that year there was a general mill stoppage throughout south-eastern Lancashire. Those on strike were determined to stop others from working, and on Friday morning the 12th of August a mob of men and women marched from Rochdale to Bacup, armed with hedge stakes and crowbars, and continued onwards towards Todmorden. Every mill en route was visited, the fires raked out and the plugs drawn from the boilers. Shopkeepers and innkeepers were forced, under threat of violence, to 'donate' bread and ale. The agitators or 'plugdrawers' visited Waterside Mill, where Fielden's operatives were actually receiving higher wages than the plugdrawers themselves demanded. No opposition was offered, but special constables were sworn in and Hussars from Burnley were quartered in Buckley's Mill at Ridgefoot. The plugdrawers marched on Halifax, where, 600 strong, they joined a contingent from Bradford the following Monday, and proceeded to attack the mills of the Bradford district.

To add to the social unrest, indeed to foment it, there was the politics of revolution — Chartism. "The People's Charter" sought to obtain many of the rights which today we take for granted, often forgetting that they were hard won. It demanded the following reforms:-

1. THE VOTE for every man over 21 years of age. (Votes for women weren't thought of in those days!)

2. A SECRET BALLOT. (Elections in the early 19th century often involved intimidation and violence.)

3. NO PROPERTY QUALIFICATION. (Opening Parliament to the common man.)

4. PAYMENT OF MEMBERS. (As above.)

5. PROPORTIONAL REPRESENTATION. (The 1832 Bill had improved things but fell far short of what needed to be done.)

6. ANNUAL PARLIAMENTS. (This has still not been achieved.)

These demands might sound reasonable to us today, but they did not seem so to the ruling classes of the early 19th century. Such ideas were regarded as subversive, and were treated accordingly. Chartism and the Plug Riots were inextricably intertwined, and so were the political aims and interests of those intent on quelling such "lawless and seditious" activities. This is not to say, however, that Chartism was made up entirely of persons from the lower classes. Chartism indeed enjoyed the support of many prominent men, the Fieldens included.

It is quite possible that John Fielden would have attended the large Chartist meeting which was held here at the Basin Stone in the August of 1842 (the same month as the Plug Riots). 1842 saw a long hot summer of strikes, agitation, violence and unrest. The great Chartist leader, Feargus O'Connor had been touring the north west, visiting such towns as Bacup, Colne and Burnley, where workers were on short time and strikes were breaking out. His fiery oratory stirred up the feelings of the poor operatives of Lancashire (indeed he described himself as the champion of the "unshorn chins, the blistered hands and fustian jackets"), and it is hardly surprising that he was eventually arrested and charged at Lancaster in 1843 with inciting the people of Lancashire to riot.

The Basin Stone, Walsden Edge.

An extract from one of O'Connor's speeches culled from the Halifax Guardian (8th October 1836) will perhaps give you an idea of the kind of oratory to which the ragged, motley crowd of locals, who assembled here at the Basin Stone to hear him speak, must have been subjected:

"You think you pay nothing? Why, it is you who pay all! It is you who pay six to eight million of taxes for keeping up the army, for what?? For keeping up the taxes!!"

It seems incredible when one tries to imagine the crowd of over a thousand people, which, in August 1842 gathered in this bleak spot to hear the speeches of Chartist leaders. One of the speakers, Robert Brooke, a lame schoolmaster, urged that men should cease working until the Charter was obtained, and that overseers should be asked for relief and some other means be adopted to obtain it. For this speech Brooke was arrested and tried at Lancaster with more than fifty other Chartists charged with uttering seditious speeches. All, however, were acquitted.

Such repression as this did not, however, stop these political rallies. A meeting was held, for example, at Pike Holes near Stoodley Pike, attended by nearly two thousand persons to protest against the non-representation of working men in Parliament, and the sum of £1 13s 6d collected, to "help to freedom" Ernest Jones, who in 1847 was to stand as M.P. for Halifax under the Chartist banner. Meetings were frequently held by torchlight in these wild and remote places, and the sight of a line of torches proceeding over dark and lonely moors must have presented a strange, half pagan sight to those who witnessed it. One section of the Chartists proposed the use of "Physical Force" — one of the Chartists' slogans proclaimed "sell thy garment and buy a sword" — and it is said that men secretly collected pikes and engaged in drill exercises on these remote Pennine uplands.

Unfortunately the 'Revolution' never came; but if Chartism itself declined, Chartist ideas and principles certainly did not, and were to play a vital role in the evolution of democracy in Britain in later years. John Fielden and his offspring "sold garments" yet declined to "take up the sword", preferring to use the pen and the spoken word in pursuit of their radical aims. The Fieldens were not, however, totally averse to the use of political violence, as we will see further along the Fielden Trail.

From the Basin Stone the path continues up the moor to Gaddings Reservoirs, a popular local resort in summer and looking across the valley, up the gorge towards Cornholme, Pendle Hill can be seen on the far horizon.

Gaddings Reservoirs

There are two reservoirs here, Easterly and Westerly Gaddings. The latter is the only one still containing any water, Easterly Gaddings having dried up and grown over long ago. These were the final supply reservoirs to be built for the Rochdale Canal, being the last of an immense complex of reservoirs and feeder channels that stretched across the moors all the way from Blackstone Edge.

Water supply had always been a problem for the Rochdale Canal, as we have already seen; and after the opening of the Manchester section of the canal the problem became even more acute. In the years leading up to 1827 a complex system of reservoirs and channels had been constructed. Altogether there were eight reservoirs. The original reservoir for the canal had been the one at Blackstone Edge, which under certain conditions washes over the moor road leading down to Cragg Vale. Afterwards came White Holme, Warland and Lighthazzles Reservoirs, Upper and Lower Chelburn Reservoirs, Hollingworth Lake and finally the twin reservoirs here at Gaddings, begun in 1824.

In order to avoid the continuing "annoyance and torment" suffered by mill owners in the Calder Valley, the canal owners agreed to build Easterly Gaddings for the sole use of the mills, to be filled once a year from the feeders on Langfield Common. Subsequently, the mill owners themselves (led by the Fieldens) reciprocated by building Westerly Gaddings alongside. This was to provide additional capacity and be a means of ensuring supply to the canal in dry periods. The supply from Gaddings ran into Lumbutts Clough, and then to the Calder, passing through the dams, goits and wheels of an assortment of mills en route, many of them (Lumbutts for example) being part of the Fielden 'Empire' of outlying spinning mills. The Fieldens, who led the mill owners' group, had a major interest in the maintaining of water supplies in the Calder Valley, and Gaddings represents a compromise drawn up between two previously warring interests.

From the 'beach' at Gaddings follow the drain towards the head of Black Clough. Across the moor ahead can be seen the embankment of the Warland Reservoir and drain, carrying the Pennine Way. If you happen to be here "in season" you will see it alive with distant walkers, and here, on this defunct and overgrown channel, snaking around the head of Black Clough, you will feel isolated and apart from them.

Before reaching the head of Black Clough, near a point where the embankment of the Gaddings drain has collapsed, turn left, following a faint, cairned path down to the stream. From the stream ascend to the cairn on Jeremy Hill, (a small knoll with a rash of stones nearby). From here pass over open moor to the summit outcrop on Coldwell Hill, recrossing the by now totally overgrown Gaddings Drain en route. Ahead can be seen Withens Clough Reservoir and the wooded hillsides above Cragg Vale. On the right, the Pennine Way approaches from the Warland Drain, a badly eroded path following a line of stakes over the moor. On joining the Pennine Way, bear left, to Withens Gate. Just follow the trail of bottles, coke cans and empty crisp packets!

At Withens Gate the Pennine Way continues onwards to Stoodley Pike Monument. My route, however, recommends a short detour from the main route in order to see the 'Te Deum Stone'. At Withens Gate, turn right along the causey, following the Calderdale Way towards Cragg Vale. Soon the route reaches a large gate in an intake wall. Climb over the stile here to find the 'Te Deum' stone on the other side of the wall.

Although the 'Te Deum' stone has no particular association with the Fieldens it is well worth the short diversion involved in order to see it. One face of this squat, ancient stone is inscribed with the letters ID and a cross, whilst on the adjacent face is the inscription 'TE DEUM LAUDAMUS' — "We praise thee O Lord!". Here, at this consecrated stone, weary travellers gave thanks and prayed for a safe journey. Also, as with the traditional 'Lych Gate', coffins were rested here on their way to burial in Heptonstall Churchyard, and no doubt prayers offered for the soul of the deceased. In those days Heptonstall was the only church in the area, and here, as in other parts of the Dales, it was by no means unusual for people to carry their dead over the moors for burial. Many so-called 'Corpse Roads' owe their origins to this necessary and time-honoured practice.

From the 'Te Deum Stone' climb back over the stile, and bear right over moorland towards quarry delfs. Beyond the quarried area the Pennine Way is rejoined. From here it is simple (but stony) stroll along the well defined path which leads to Stoodley Pike Monument (which is one of those places that never seems to get any nearer!).

Stoodley Pike Monument

Stoodley Pike Monument, standing at 1310 feet above sea level is the highest point reached by the Fielden Trail. It is also the coldest, bleakest and wildest point! The Pike appears to be welcoming, yet

Stoodley Pike Monument

when you get there you soon find that it offers little in the way of shelter from the elements. After groping your way through pitch darkness up the staircase to reach the viewing platform, you find that it's actually colder in the Pike than it was at ground level, where you at least had stone buttresses to break the wind. On a wet, cold and windy day, with grey clouds billowing over the moors, Stoodley Pike can be a miserable place indeed.

Stoodley Pike has been in existence much longer than the rather lugubrious egyptian monument that crowns it. In 1274 Stoodley was mentioned in the Wakefield Manor Court Rolls, and it seems fairly certain that originally a large cairn stood on the Pike, probably covering an ancient burial, for tradition asserts that a skeleton was found on the spot when the first Monument was constructed in 1814.

The first Stoodley Pike Monument was constructed by public subscription to commemorate the surrender of Paris to the Allies in March 1814. Among the names associated with its construction we find Greenwoods, Halsteads, Lacys, Inghams and, of course, Fieldens. The foundation stone was laid with Masonic honours and a feast and celebration held. The completed Monument was 37 yds. 2 ft. 4 in. high. For the first 5 yds. it was square, above which height the structure was circular, tapering to the top. Inside, a staircase of around 150 precarious steps led to the top where there was a small room with a fireplace. While work was continuing on the monument, Napoleon escaped from Elba and finally met his 'Waterloo', and it was in that year, 1815, that the monument was finally completed.

Its career was ill-starred. Within a few years it had suffered vandalism, and the entrance had been walled up. Nemesis arrived on February 8th 1854 when, during the afternoon, after a rumbling which startled the entire neighbourhood, it was discovered that the Monument had collapsed. By an unhappy co-incidence this happened on the same afternoon that the Russian Ambassador left London before the declaration of war with Russia. As a result of this, Stoodley Pike Monument has since been saddled with the myth that its collapse heralds the approach of war.

On March 10th 1854 a meeting was held at the Golden Lion in Todmorden with John Fielden in the chair. Object — to rebuild the Monument. John's brother, Samuel Fielden, was also among the speakers at the meeting. It was estimated that the rebuilding would cost between £300 and £400. On March 30th another meeting was held and it was decided, on the motion of Samuel Fielden, that the Monument should take its present obelisk form. The Fieldens, Sam, John and Joshua, contributed to the project along with other local worthies, and £300 was raised. On June 1st they held another meeting, at which designs were submitted for the new Monument, resulting in the acceptance of the design of local architect Mr. James Green of Portsmouth, Todmorden. A Committee of Works was appointed:

Chairman — John Fielden of Dobroyd.

Treasurer — Samuel Fielden of Centre Vale.

J. Ingham, Joshua Fielden of Stansfield Hall, John Eastwood, Edward Lord, John Veevers, Wm. Greenwood of Stones, J. Green (architect), John Lacy and Mr. Knowles of Lumb (secretary).

By now £600 had been raised, helped by subscriptions from Thomas Fielden of Crumpsall, Manchester, and Mrs. James Fielden of Dobroyd. In the end the total bill came to over £812 with £212 outstanding. This debt was generously liquidated by (guess who!) Mr. Samuel Fielden of Centre Vale.

Thus it was that in 1856, the year of the Peace (Crimean War) the Monument was reconstructed in its present form. Within a few years the fabric was in need of repair, and when this work was carried out in 1889, again assisted by funding from John and Samuel Fielden, improvements were made — among them more adequate lighting for the staircase and a lightning conductor. Once again, costs exceeded estimates, and once again Fieldens cleared the debt. The emblems and inscriptions over the entrance to the monument were carved by Mr. Luke Fielden, and it is believed that John Fielden himself composed the inscription. The lettering is not too easy to read these days, so I will save you the trouble:-

"STOODLEY PIKE
A PEACE MONUMENT
Erected by Public Subscription.
Commenced in 1814 to commemorate the Surrender of Paris to the Allies and finished after the Battle of Waterloo when peace was established in 1815. By a strange co-incidence the Pike fell on the day the Russian Ambassador left London before the declaration of war with Russia in 1854 and it was rebuilt when peace was proclaimed in 1856. Repaired and lightning conductor fixed 1889."

What of the Pike today? If you can find a pleasant enough day to visit this bleak spot, the views are excellent, ranging from Holme Moss and Emley Moor to the south and Boulsworth Hill and the Haworth moors to the north. Less far afield we can see right into the heart of Todmorden and up the gorge towards Cornholme and Hartley Royd. Immediately below, the main Burnley Road can be seen through a gap in the hills, passing through the vicinity of Eastwood. It is incredible to think that it was somewhere down there, near Callis Bridge, that James Shepherd rescued the little boy, Samuel S. Fielden, from the raging river, after he had been swept there all the way from the centre of Todmorden. No wonder the poor boy did not survive his ordeal!

Stoodley Pike Monument belongs to Todmorden, despite being perhaps nearer to Hebden Bridge. The Pike is not visible from Hebden Bridge, whereas it dominates Todmorden from a distance and can be seen from every part of the town. It is not for nothing that the Monument is displayed in Todmorden's Coat-of-Arms. Yet it is not unique. The strange compulsion that led 19th century Yorkshiremen and Lancashire folk to build bizarre 'follies' on their hilltops is something of a mystery. A tradition was established that in an odd, and more functional, kind of way has persisted into the 20th century with the masts and towers of Holme Moss and Emley Moor, not to mention the host of smaller TV booster transmitters to be found on hillsides all over the area. Yet the old 'follies' — Wainhouse Tower, The Pecket Memorial, Rivington Pike, the Earl Crag Monuments

The View from Stoodley Pike.

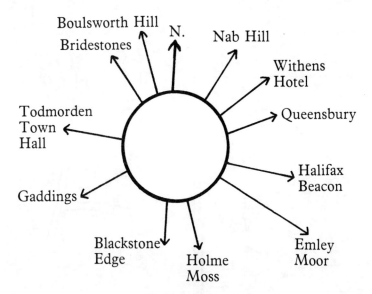

Stoodley Pike to Todmorden

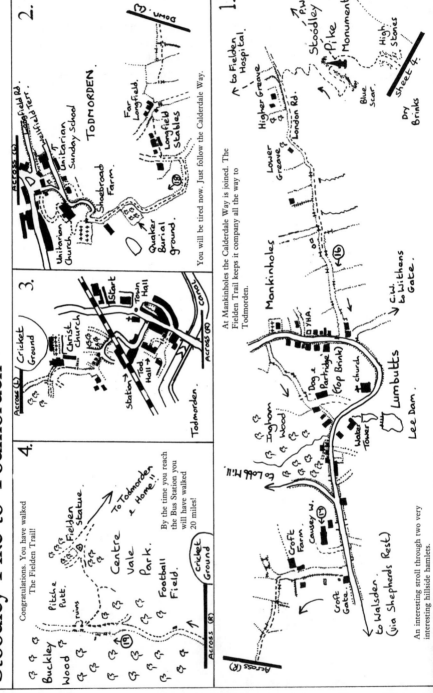

1.

P.W. Stoodley Pike Monument. Blue Scar. High Stones. Dry Brinks. Sheet 4.

← to Fielden Hospital.

Higher Greave. Lower Greave. London Rd. Mankinholes. YHA. c.w. to Withens Gate. Dog & Partridge (Top Brink). t church. Ingham Wood. Water Tower. Lee Dam. Lumbutts. Lob Mill. Causey W. Croft Farm. Croft Gate. ← to Walsden. (via Shepherds Rest)

An interesting stroll through two very interesting hillside hamlets.

At Mankinholes the Calderdale Way is joined. The Fielden Trail keeps it company all the way to Todmorden.

2.

Scaitcliffe Rd. Scaitcliffe Terr. Unitarian Sunday School. TODMORDEN. Unitarian Church. Quaker Burial Ground. Sheebroad Farm. Far Longfield. Longfield Stables.

Down 3.

You will be tired now. Just follow the Calderdale Way.

3.

Cricket Ground. Christ Church. Start. Town Hall. Station. Tod Hall. Todmorden. Canal. Across (6)

4.

Congratulations. You have walked The Fielden Trail!

Buckley Wood. ruins. Pitch & Putt. Fielden Statue. To Todmorden & Home!! Centre Vale Park. Football Field. Cricket Ground.

By the time you reach the Bus Station you will have walked 20 miles!

near Keighley, Wainman's Pinnacle and Lund's Tower, the Jubilee Tower on Almondbury at Huddersfield — all bear mute testimony to this strange urge. Perhaps it is similar to the one which prompts lesser mortals to add stones to cairns on the Pennine Way. Who knows?

It is time to move on. If you are feeling really energetic you can follow the Pennine Way to Kirk Yetholm. If you are following the Fielden Trail, however, you will ignore such temptations and head back towards Todmorden.

From the entrance to the Monument walk straight forwards towards the edge of the scarp, bearing slightly left. Soon a path can be seen descending the steep face of the hillside towards a cluster of hospital buildings on the 'shelf' below. This is the Fielden Hospital, which was built at Leebottom in 1892 by John Ashton Fielden, who was carrying out the wishes of his father, the late Mr. Samuel Fielden of Centre Vale. Samuel had long displayed an interest in the welfare of children and the building of a children's hospital had always been his dearest wish.

Near the end of the Fielden Trail at Centre Vale Park is the Fielden School of Art. This was originally built and maintained as an elementary school at Samuel's own private expense. His wife, Sarah Jane, was particularly notable in this respect. She was the daughter of Joseph Brookes Yates of Liverpool, (Samuel married her at Childwall Church near to that town in 1859), and no doubt she would have been quite familiar with the conditions endured by the slum children of that sleazy, bustling port. All this may be speculation, but even if she was not influenced by such realities, her interest in the welfare of Todmorden's children is in no doubt. In August 1874 the first School Board in the Todmorden district was elected and Mrs. Fielden was its most distinguished and active member. She devoted many years to the study of the education of younger children, at first in unpretentious buildings in Cobden St., then later in her own school at Centre Vale, where she engaged in education work along lines which she herself had searched out and practically tested. (Centre Vale School continued until 1896).

But back to the Fielden Trail. The path from Stoodley Pike passes steeply down to the left through Red Scar and after meandering down the moor eventually reaches London Road near Higher Greave. Bear left, following this track to Mankinholes.

Further down the hillside below London Road is yet another hospital, Stansfield View. This was originally the Union Workhouse, although it wasn't constructed until the 1870s (the original Poor Law Amendment Act having been passed in 1834). The reason for the delay was the fierce and often violent opposition to this despised institution, an opposition in which the Fieldens were particularly vociferous and active. Events in Mankinholes in 1838 were to have a particular impact on the area and delay the implementation of the new Poor Law for many years.

Descending slightly, the walled lane emerges on the metalled road leading to Lumbutts at the southern end of Mankinholes village. Beyond Lumbutts this road connects with the Salter Rake Gate we passed over earlier on the Fielden Trail. At the end of London Road turn right into Mankinholes village. On the right is a beautifully designed stone trough which was constructed as a watering place for the packhorse trains, which at one time were the almost universal traffic of the area. It is hard to imagine that in the centuries prior to the Industrial Revolution this sleepy little community lay astride what was then a busy trade route.

Mankinholes

... IS DELIGHTFUL! Apart from the tarmac lane which brings the odd speeding motorist through its meandering, tree-shaded heart, Mankinholes is venerable and peaceful, a community that time seems to have passed by. It is tempting to call the place "pre-industrial", but more accurate to call it "pre-Industrial Revolution", for although mills, canals, towns and railways have left Mankinholes alone on the hillside with its memories, it was nevertheless, in the days of its prosperity, almost entirely given over to the domestic textile industry. Even with the Industrial Revolution, textiles did not die out up here, as the traditional domestic woollen industry was simply replaced by Fielden's cotton spinning mill at nearby Lumbutts, just a little further along the hillside. Up here on the 'shelf' of land just below Stoodley Pike we are given the rare opportunity of seeing two small and different industrial communities side by side — the one domestic and the other factory based — representing two different epochs in the history of the area.

In Mankinholes we see the earlier epoch. A woollen industry characterised by the spinning wheel and the handloom, the jingling packhorses and their colourful drivers, the "broggers". When Defoe passed through this area in the 18th century, he remarked upon the 'pieces' of cloth which could be seen on every hillside, stretched upon their tenter frames (the origin of the expression 'on tenter hooks'). Weavers would often carry pieces to market on their backs as we have seen. Besides the weavers there were the croppers with their enormous shears for cutting the nap on the cloth; there were dyers, fullers with their stocks and waterwheels, their tiny mills serving an industry centred on the hillfarmer's hearth and home, yet pointing towards the new industrial age that was to come, for in the end the 'hearth and home' would come to serve the mill and the flow of progress would create new communities and environments, leaving the time honoured industries of communities like Mankinholes high and dry.

So Mankinholes remains aloof and detached from the bustle below, nursing its memories, a community put out to pasture. Mankinholes, like other places we have encountered along the route, was a stronghold of early Quakerism, the first recorded meetings in the area being held here at the house of Joshua Laycock, to which a burial ground was attached on December 3rd 1667. Half a little croft called 'Tenter Croft' was rented as a burial ground at a yearly rent of 'one twopence of silver' for a term of 900 years. This plot of ground still forms part of one of the farms at the northern end of the village, and on one of the outbuildings is a gravestone with the inscription "J.S. 1685". Within a short time of the passing of the Toleration Act in 1689, Quaker Meeting Houses were registered in Haworth, Mankinholes, Bottomley and Todmorden. Eventually, as the development of the area began to centre on the valley below, the Quakers moved nearer to Todmorden — to Shoebroad and ultimately to Cockpit Hill behind Fielden Square in Todmorden.

With the end of the Quaker persecutions, Mankinholes returned to its tranquil life. In the wake of the Quakers came the Methodists, who built a chapel here in 1815, and in the same year a school was opened with Mr. William Bayes of Lumbutts as headmaster. As the cotton spinning industry developed at nearby Lumbutts, the traditional domestic industries of Mankinholes declined, and this little community might simply have passed into oblivion and obscurity had it not been for the sudden and extremely violent scenes which took place here on the afternoon of Friday November 16th 1838, events which were to have a profound effect on the neighbourhood for some years to come.

These troubles were caused by the Poor Law Amendment Act of 1834, which abolished the old system of parish relief for the poor which dated back to the time of Elizabeth I, and brought in a new regime, administered by three commissioners who rapidly became known as the 'Three Bashaws (Pashas) of Somerset House'. These commissioners were empowered to group parishes into Unions where workhouses (which came to be called Unions) would be established.

As a result of this, the able-bodied might receive no relief except within the workhouse, where conditions were deliberately made harsh. In the workhouse men and women were kept apart to prevent childbearing, and to enter it meant leaving one's home and loved ones to suffer perpetual imprisonment simply for having the misfortune to be poor or unemployed.

In the south the new act was quickly implemented, but in the north it was resolutely and often violently opposed. "The New Bastilles" as the workhouses were called, were set on fire or pulled down; and in many northern towns it was many years before the act could be enforced. To understand the reason for this violent opposition we must look more closely at the objects and aims of the act, and at the social and economic differences between the northern and southern regions.

Mankinholes.

The aim of the Poor Law Amendment Act was primarily to reduce vagrancy by making it impossible for the poor to get an easy living by "scrounging" off the parish. In certain areas this situation was indeed the case — with many people preferring to live on relief rather than seek honest employment. It was reasoned that the introduction of this new system would make living "on the Parish" so harsh, restrictive and unpleasant that a man would take on any kind of work rather than submit himself to the horrors of the workhouse.

The implementation of the law proved that there had indeed been some point to the argument. The numbers of people seeking relief dropped drastically in the south, but unfortunately the government of the day completely misjudged the effects of the new Poor Law upon the industrial north, where a completely different situation was to be found.

In the north things were different. Work was centred on the new factories and the factories were having difficult times. Traditional industries like handloom weaving were in decline, and in factories with the new machines fewer hands were needed to do the work of many. Wages were poor and unemployment was widespread. Naturally enough, the arrival of the workhouse upon the scene proved to be the last straw. In the south it may have persuaded the 'idle poor' to seek work, but in the north there was often no work of any kind to be had, especially in areas where the whole community was often entirely dependent on a single industry, or even a single employer. People were forced to enter the workhouse through no fault of their own and be separated from their loved ones with no prospects save harsh labour and perpetual imprisonment. Furthermore, the workhouse initiated a downward spiral, for if work was available, the poor, rather than submit to the rigours of the workhouse and the workhouse test and lose their homes, would accept lower wages and longer hours and thus aggravate still further the great struggle with poverty in which so many of the weavers and workers were at that time engaged.

Lower wages and longer hours would, of course, benefit the mill masters, giving them an endless supply of cheap labour, but thankfully there were those more enlightened souls who were aware of the injustice of the new Poor Law, and who were ready to organise local opposition to the hated workhouse.

In Yorkshire there were two hotbeds of Poor Law opposition — Huddersfield, led by Richard Oastler, and the workers of Todmorden, led by 'Honest John' Fielden. On May 13th 1837 'Honest John' was speaker at a huge West Riding anti-Poor Law rally held on Hartshead

Moor near Liversedge, and on 19th February 1838 he became vice chairman of Earl Stanhope's Anti-Poor Law Association. The struggle against the workhouse in Todmorden was bitter. Elections of 18 Guardians for the seven townships in the Union were ordered in January 1837, but Todmorden, Walsden and Langfield refused to proceed, and when the Guardians did meet on 6th July 1838, their opponents forced them to adjourn. As regards John Fielden's involvement in these events, his opposition was vigorous: "A most extraordinary course of conduct was pursued by Messrs. Fielden & Co.," who dismissed all their workers to overload the system and force the Guardians to resign. Unfortunately they "wholly failed in this remarkable endeavour to intimidate the Guardians" and re-opened their works within days, on the 16th. John then warned the Guardians with an ominous placard:

> "To oppose force we are not yet prepared, but if the people of this and surrounding districts are to be driven to the alternative of either doing so, or surrendering their local government into the hands of an unconstitutional board of lawmakers, the time may not be far distant when the experiment may be tried, and I would warn those who provoke the people to such a combat of the danger they are incurring."

The warning was duly noted and the Guardians were at first cautious, not attempting to implement the Act fully for some time. But attempts to levy rates through the Todmorden and Langfield Overseers led to tangled legal actions, and when two Constables were sent from Halifax to Mankinholes to seize the household goods of Mr. William Ingham, the Overseer, for his refusal on behalf of the township of Langfield to pay the new Poor Law levy, they could not have been aware of the seething cauldron of violent resentment that they were about to overturn.

What happened next is best expressed in the words of the time, from a pamphlet account published in 1838:-

"The Overseer of Todmorden, Mr. Ingham, has recently had a fine imposed upon him for neglecting to pay the demands made upon him under the new [Poor] Law. In consequence a distress warrant was taken out against him on 8th December Thursday. Feather, the Under Deputy and King, Sergeant of the Watch proceeded to Langfield to mark the goods and give the usual notice that if the fine was not paid the goods would be taken and sold . . . On Friday 16th May they went, taking with them a horse and a cart . . . Immediately upon the Officers being seen, a woman, who was standing with several others upon a piece of rising ground at a short distance called out. "Ring the 'larum bell", she repeated, and forthwith a bell commenced ringing . . . with tremendous violence. In almost an instant the bell of Mr. Fielden's factory situated at Lumbutts about two fields length from Ingham's house was set a ringing and was followed by several others. These bells were rung from 10 to 15 minutes incessantly.

The game was now commenced, factories emptied of men armed with clubs, etc., hastening to the scene of action. Soon there was a mob of two thousand people gathered!"

The mob threatened to raze his house if Ingham would not deliver up the Constables, who, after having been mauled by the mob, were now hiding in Ingham's house. Eventually, however, an agreement was reached whereby the Officers agreed to take an oath that they would not return here again on such an errand. The mob was now slightly pacified — but not content with this they demanded that the Constables should apologise on their knees. Neither Officer was willing to submit to this kind of degradation, so when Ingham finally opened the door "both Officers were seized in an instant and the mob commenced stripping them of their clothes. Feather, now seeing the position they were in, begged for mercy. The mob shouted: 'we will spare your lives! Mr. Fielden told us to spare your lives!'"

Left now to the mercies of the mob the Officers were "most severely kicked, thrown upon the ground, dragged by their heels upon the ground and suffered the most murderous treatment. Their hats were taken off, filled with mud, and then with great violence forced over their faces. Thus blinded and choked they continued to make their way towards Stoodley Bridge." Half a dozen of the mob protected them for a time, but, being attacked by the remainder, they left them to their fate.

Upon arriving at the last turn in Stoodley Plantation the mob threatened to throw them into the canal: "One man who was holding King's left arm said — 'Now if you will make a split [run] I will give you a chance!' [They were about forty yards away from the canal]. He [King] did so but was immediately pursued by the man who had hold of his right arm. This fellow, who King says was one of Mr. Fielden's mechanics, proved to be a treacherous rogue who tried to pitch him into the cut . . ." The Officers eventually found refuge at a Mr. Oliver's, and managed to get some clothes and catch the 'Perseverance' Mail Coach back to Halifax (their cart having been smashed and burned and the horse turned loose by the mob).

That might have been an end to it, but on the following Wednesday, (21st November), a rumour spread to the effect that the Constables were returning once more, this time with a body of soldiers. The balloon went up and the mob gathered; but the rumour turned out to be a damp squib. Not to be thwarted however:

"The infuriated mob determined to manifest their indignation at the new Poor Law and its advocates in the following summary manner — From Mankinholes they proceeded to Mutterhole, the residence of Mr. Royston Oliver, one of the Poor Law Guardians, and broke the whole of his windows and doors; after which they proceeded to Wood Mill, breaking the windows of Mr. Samuel Oliver's house, and the windows of the inn where the Guardians hold their meetings."

From here the mob went "then to Stones Wood, the residence of Messrs. Ormerod Bros., destroying windows, doors and furniture, and on their return called on Mr. Helliwell of Friths Mill." The mob then went to Wattey Place (Wm. Greenwood), Jeremiah Oliver (the surgeon) and the house of Miss Holt, the draper, whose windows were smashed. Also suffering damage were the houses of Mr. Henry Atkinson (shoemaker) and Mr. Stansfield, Solicitor and Clerk to the Board of Guardians.

On reaching Todmorden Hall, which was at this time the residence of James Taylor Esq, the Magistrate, they destroyed windows, doors, furniture, family paintings and carriages, and carried off spirits, wines and the contents of the cellar. Next they went to the house of Mr. James Suthers, who lived up Blind Lane and who was the Collecting Overseer under the new Poor Law for the Todmorden District. Here again, windows were smashed and the house plundered, and the mob would have made a bonfire of the furniture but for the appeal of a lady nearby who feared for the houses catching fire; so instead they threw it into the nearby watercourse. The mob ended its rampage at the residence of Mr. Greenwood at Hare Hill, where, after breaking windows and doors they set the house on fire, which was quickly extinguished by a fire engine sent from Fielden's Mill at Waterside before much damage was done. All the people whose houses were attacked were either Union officials or "other persons supposed to be friendly to the Law"; Miss Holt for example, whose windows disappeared under the vengeance of the mob, was sister-in-law to Joshua Fielden, but had shown herself by chatter over her shop counter to be in favour of the new Poor Law.

Retribution was swift. Soldiers were brought in and large numbers of Fielden's workers were arrested by police and troops. Of 40 men tried however, only one was actually imprisoned. The Fieldens and their workers had won — it was not until 1877 that Todmorden finally agreed to build a workhouse.

After these events Mankinholes reverted back to its former tranquility (although it must have seen a little activity four years later with the Chartist and Anti-Corn Law disturbances). Mr. Ingham's house still remains, standing in a cluster of trees in Mankinholes with its gable to the road. It seems hard to imagine the scenes that took place here on that fateful Friday afternoon in 1838. Such violence seems somehow incongruous in this gentle place.

But back to the present. From Mankinholes the Fielden Trail follows the route of the Calderdale Way into Todmorden, via Lumbutts. Just beyond the northern end of the village the Wesleyan Methodist Sunday School appears on the right. This was built by public subscription in 1833. The adjoining ground was the site of Mankinholes Methodist Church, and a sign by the gate informs us that it was "built in 1814, enlarged in 1870, rebuilt in 1911 and closed in 1979." Opposite the chapel gate a paved track leads between walls to the Dog and Partridge or Top Brink Inn at Lumbutts, one of the oldest hostelries in the district. Sheep fairs were once held here, and business deals clinched over a pint of ale. The Langfield Moor Gateholders met here and the pub was a traditional haunt of the 'Broggers' (the packhorse men).

Before reaching the front of the Top Brink, a cobbled ginnel leads down to the Lumbutts Road near the water tower. Turn right here: soon a stream passes beneath the road and an imposing mill-house appears on the left in front of the water tower. This house, and the tower, is all that remains of Fielden's Spinning Mill. Around this mill in the 19th century mushroomed the cotton manufacturing community of Lumbutts.

Lumbutts

Sited on the fast flowing stream flowing down Black Clough from Langfield Common, Lumbutts was the ideal site for the development of a small manufacturing community of the Industrial Revolution. Whereas Mankinholes owed its livelihood to farming and to the domestic-based textiles of an earlier age, Lumbutts, in contrast, was almost entirely created by, and centred around, its cotton mill; which was one of the many remote outposts of the Fielden's cotton manufacturing 'empire'. Nearly all of its 200 or so inhabitants were employed by Fieldens in the 19th century.

The mill that stood in front of the huge tower was (on the authority of a local retired postman I conversed with) Fielden's Scutching and

Carding Department. On the other side of the road stood the Spinning Shed. Today only the water tower, the dams that fed it, the manager's house, and some workers' cottages remain to testify to the substantial manufacturing establishment that developed here. The water tower especially was a fine work of engineering. In its day it housed three overshot waterwheels which were fed from the dams up Black Clough. The three wheels were arranged in a vertical sequence so that each wheel had its own feed, but was also driven by the water falling from the wheel above it. The top water fell a total distance of 90 feet and the whole system was capable of generating 54 horse power. Today, though ruined, the tower is still a fascinating structure and is a landmark visible from all the surrounding moorland edges.

From Lumbutts follow the metalled road onwards towards the Shepherd's Rest. On this tarmac road we are, in fact, walking along part of the Salter Rake Gate. A little further along, near the pub, the old stone causey coming down from the moors joins up with the modern road, where it disappears beneath the tarmac. The Fielden Trail however, leaves the road before reaching this point.

After passing 'Causey West' on the right, turn right by pole no. 215 at Croft Gate to Croft Farm. Just beyond Croft Farm pass through a stile and follow the footpath to Far Longfield Farm. (Look for the Calderdale Way waymarks). The Shepherd's Rest and the road can be seen across fields on the left.

At Far Longfield, go through a stile by pole no. 273, following the path through Longfield Stables to a farm road beyond which llamas may sometimes be seen grazing. (Yes, I did say llamas!). On reaching a junction of farm roads a small dam appears in the field opposite. Turn right, following a walled lane to:-

Shoebroad Quaker Burial Ground

If you wish to explore this place more closely it will be necessary for you to shin over the wall, as the entrance gate was walled up long ago. The exercise is hardly worth the effort, however, as apart from a few gravestones belonging to the Oddy family, there is really nothing there to see. This is a Quaker Burial Ground, and Quakers were not allowed headstones or grave monuments until relatively recent times, the tradition being one of anonymous burial in an unmarked plot of ground. It might come as rather a surprise therefore, when I tell you that there are at least 24 Quaker Fieldens buried in this tiny plot of ground, and goodness knows how many other people from other

Quaker families in the district. Here lie the mortal remains of Joshua Fielden (I) of Bottomley, who along with his brother John Fielden of Hartley Royd, were amongst the first people in the district to become Quakers. He was buried here on 21st April 1693, and was followed by successive Joshuas, the last Joshua being 'Honest John's' father, the enterprising Joshua Fielden (IV) of Edge End and later Waterside, who was buried here in April 1811. The last Fielden to be buried here was old Joshua's youngest surviving daughter, Salley Fielden, who died at Waterside on 18th September 1859 aged 79. (She was Mary Fielden's aunt.) Also buried here are John and Tamar Fielden of Todmorden Hall, whom we will shortly encounter on the last lap of the Fielden Trail.

From the Quaker cemetery the track continues to descend towards Todmorden, passing Shoebroad Farm (another Quaker meeting place) on the left. On reaching the bend at Honey Hole, do not follow it, but instead continue onwards through an iron gate which leads into the cemetery. The gravel path turns left, descends through trees and shrubbery and finally emerges at the chancel end of Todmorden Unitarian Church. On the left, at the corner of the church, are the graves of Samuel and Joshua Fielden, two of the three brothers who left such a lasting mark on the architectural character of Todmorden. (The third brother, John Fielden J.P. of Dobroyd Castle, is buried at Grimston Park near Leeds.) Also buried here is Samuel Fielden's wife, Sarah Jane, whose educational works were recently discussed. The inscription tells us that she was born at West Dingle, Liverpool, on 5th November 1819 and died at Centre Vale in 1910. There is less inscription on Joshua's grave, although we note with some surprise that Joshua, by a strange twist of fate, died on his 70th birthday, being born on March 8th 1827 and dying on the same date in 1897. My first visit here seemed a rather haunting experience. There I stood, with one of Samuel Fielden's letters in my pocket, along with correspondence written by his sister Mary. It was strange to reflect that had fate not brought this material into my possession, I would not even have been aware of his existence, still less visited his grave. It was equally strange to think that his birthday was the same as my own, 21st January. For me, my own personal Fielden Trail began right here.

From the two graves, bear right, around the front of the church, passing through the magnificent porch beneath the tall spired tower. In the mosaic pavement is a small, circular device containing the names of Samuel, Joshua and John Fielden. On reaching the far end of the building, bear right, to where the main entrance to the church stands near a magnificent 'rose' window.

Todmorden Unitarian Church

Todmorden Unitarian Church was built by the three Fielden
Brothers, John, Samuel and Joshua, in memory of their famous father,
'Honest John' Fielden M.P. The first sod was cut in April 1865, and
the corner stone was laid by Samuel Fielden on December 23rd 1865.
Prior to its opening the structure was complete in almost every detail,
and the gathering of 800 people who met for the offical opening on
April 7th 1869 saw the church as a finished work of art. Like most of
the Fielden buildings in Todmorden the Unitarian Church was
designed by the Westminster architect John Gibson, who created a
Gothic style church of remarkably fine taste. (Victorian 'Gothick' was
very often quite the opposite.)

"Internally this massive church, constructed in stone, marble and
oak, is 128 feet long and 46 feet wide. The magnificent spire is 196
feet in height. To ensure its safety the steeple has its foundations 30
feet down into the ground, and the pinnacles increase the stability of
the tower by their downward thrust. The lofty nave with its two aisles
has seven pointed and moulded arches on each side, springing from
pillars of Devon marble six feet in circumference. Each window in the
nave has its arch finished with the carving of a human, alternately
male and female. A unique feature of its oak roof is the insertion of a
number of small windows admitting light. These cannot be seen from
the outside. On the south side of the chancel is the vestry, originally
planned as a mortuary chapel, and on the north side is the organ
chamber and original vestry. The rose window at the western end of
the nave is one of the finest features of the church. In some lights the
35,000 pieces of glass used in its design gleam like a precious jewel.
The only other windows of stained glass are those in the chancel,
which contain representations of biblical incidents. These windows,
with colours rich and glowing, were the work of M. Capronnier of
Brussels. The beauty of this church has not been spoiled by the
addition of unsuitable memorials. It contains only four, one to the
memory of those members who gave their lives in the Great War
1914-18, and the other three to the Fielden brothers by whose
munificence the church was built . . ."

So much for the "guide book" details. Now to the sad reality. On
my second visit here I was lucky enough to arrive when the custodian
of the church, Mr. Rushworth, was showing round an architect and a
surveyor from London, who had been requested to come and inspect
the fabric, judge what repairs were necessary, and estimate the cost.
Mr. Rushworth explained to me that the church is normally locked

because of repeated acts of vandalism carried out by the youth of the neighbourhood. Only recently the church had been broken into and a lot of damage done. My guide informed me that he had once worked as a secretary at Fielden's Mill. He showed me pews at the front of the church which were slightly larger and more comfortable than the others (I wouldn't have noticed the difference had it not been pointed out to me). These were obviously the Fieldens' own private pews.

Unfortunately the future prospects for this beautiful building are none to good. Not only has the church been vandalised, but the lead on the roof has become so decayed that it is raining in, with resultant damage to the church's fabric. Mr. Rushworth informed me at the time that they had put in for a grant to restore the church, but did not feel that it would be of much use, as the cost that was estimated for the repair work was in excess of £50,000 (it only cost £36,000 to build).

Sad to say, this magnificently beautiful building is today something of a white elephant. Built in an age of Victorian wealth and opulence, the Fielden brothers would never have imagined that perhaps one day future Unitarians might be quite unable to keep up to this grandiose memorial to their father's memory. Its very scale and magnificence denies it any use other than that for which it was intended. If it were smaller, and older, there would be lots of potential uses and sources of revenue to ensure its continued survival. Alas, this is not the case. It remains, a massive, decaying church with only a small congregation.

The irony of the situation is that a few years ago, when faced with the choice of selling either the old Sunday School or the church, they sold the former on the grounds that it would be unthinkable to part with the magnificent latter building. The Sunday School (which was the original Unitarian Chapel) is now a workshop and the Unitarians are beginning to regret that they sold it. It was smaller, more adaptable and historically of greater significance than its more magnificent yet less venerable successor. There would have been far less difficulty in attracting funds to restore and modernise it. Now, alas, they are left with an unspoilt, unaltered, architecturally beautiful 'white elephant', and an enormous financial headache. There is light at the end of the tunnel though; at the time of writing, a grant has been obtained, and there are plans currently afoot to turn the church into a Fielden museum and exhibition centre. Hopefully they will succeed and Todmorden Unitarian Church may be rescued from oblivion before it is too late.

From the entrance porch of the church return to Honey Hole Road and pass Meeting House Cottage on the right. Here was the Banktop Quaker Meeting House which was built in 1808 after the meeting

house at Shoebroad had been taken down. A little further on, near a
high wall and a trough on the right, bear left past modern railings to
an iron gate in a stone wall. This leads into the graveyard of
Todmorden Unitarian Sunday School:-

Todmorden Unitarian Sunday School

The first thing we encounter at the old Sunday School is 'Honest
John' Fielden's grave, which lies almost at your feet as you enter the
graveyard. It is substantial but plain, being little more than a large
expanse of gravel surrounded by four kerbstones.

Why, you might ask, was this relatively humble spot chosen as the
last resting place of such a distinguished man as 'Honest John'
Fielden? Surely it would have been more fitting to inter his remains in
a more suitably grandiose tomb, sited in the magnificent church that
was erected nearby to his memory? The reason is simple. The Old
Sunday School was the original seat of Unitarian worship in the area
and was the building that 'Honest John' knew and loved during his
lifetime. Indeed, 'Honest John' Fielden's role in the development of
the Unitarian Faith in Todmorden cannot be ignored, for without his
enthusiasm and support that faith might well have foundered and
passed into oblivion.

The story of local Unitarianism begins in 1806 with a schism among
Methodists in the Rochdale area. This was caused by the expulsion
from his ministry of the Reverend Joseph Cooke, who was removed
from the Rochdale Methodist Circuit on account of his heretical
opinions. Joseph Cooke was both young and popular, and his
expulsion caused a secession from the ranks of Methodists in
Rochdale, Padiham, Burnley and Todmorden, which were the areas
where Cooke preached. These people gathered into Bible Reading
Societies known as "Cookite" Congregations. Cooke's friends built
for him the Providence Chapel in Clover Street, Rochdale, from
which centre he established a 'circuit' and ministered to the various
Cookite groups in neighbouring towns and villages. He died in 1811
aged 35. After his death Cookite numbers dwindled and those that
remained became known as Methodist-Unitarians, and it was to one
such group, in Todmorden, to which John Fielden, the Quaker, was
attracted.

In 1818 the renowned Unitarian Missionary, the Revd. Richard
Wright, preached at Clover Street when some Todmorden hearers
were present. They invited him to come and preach in Todmorden,

and when he did so the local Cookite group were deeply impressed, realising that Unitarianism and their own beliefs were pretty much in agreement. Equally impressed by his meeting with Richard Wright was John Fielden, the Quaker millowner, who was converted to Unitarianism as a result. Already renowned for his sincerity, ability and work as an educationalist, John Fielden was the natural choice to lead this small band of Todmorden Unitarians, and the first result of Wright's visit was the formation of the group into a "Unitarian Society", with 'Honest John' as its most influential member. Fielden invited local Unitarian Ministers to visit Todmorden on a fortnightly basis and was successful in his endeavour. The Society at first met in a meeting room at Hanging Ditch, but, as they prospered and grew in number they resolved to build a Meeting House "Where the worship of God in one Person shall be carried on and a school taught."

Thus it was that in 1824 the Todmorden Unitarian Chapel (which later became the Sunday School) was opened on Cockpit Hill, with an outstanding debt of about £500. Times were hard for the cotton operatives who were the main support of the chapel. The trustees, finding the situation a burden, begged to be relieved of the office. 'Honest John', in typical Fielden fashion solved the problem by buying the Chapel, School and all accoutrements for £480. He appointed a regular Minister and paid his salary. This Minister was to also act as Schoolmaster in 'Honest John's' own Factory School at Waterside, which we encountered earlier in our travels. 'Honest John' superintended the Sunday School in person, beginning at 9.30 am with prayers, service, and scripture reading; followed by the 'three Rs', spelling and history. From 1828 onwards Fielden provided a day school with accomodation for 100 children between the age of four and the time of going to work. A fee of 2d per week was charged. This covered the cost of materials, the teacher's salaries being paid by 'Honest John'.

On 29th May 1849, after a distinguished but alas rather brief Parliamentary career, 'Honest John' Fielden died at Skeynes in Kent and was brought to Todmorden to be buried in the yard of the chapel he had loved so well. The funeral took place on 4th June, and according to the account published in the Ashton Chronicle, it was quite a substantial affair:

"The remains of Mr. John Fielden of Centre Vale, late M.P. for Oldham, were interred on Monday in his own chapel yard at Honey Hole. The funeral procession began to move from Centre Vale about 12 o'clock, headed by the minister, Mr. James Taylor and the Revd. J. Wilkinson of Rochdale, followed by the principal gentlemen of the neighbourhood . . . The hearse was followed by two mourning coaches containing his sons and brothers . . . these were followed by four other coaches, with relatives and intimate acquaintances, among whom were Mr. Charles Hindley, M.P. for Ashton, and Mr. John and Mr. James Cobbett. These were followed by a large procession of gentlemen and operatives from Oldham, Bolton and Manchester, who had come unsolicited to pay a mark of respect to their friend and benefactor. The road was lined with spectators from . . . Centre Vale to the chapel, and thousands were on the hillsides and the tops of houses to witness the sad procession."

After 'Honest John's' death his three sons and their wives took over leadership of the Unitarian Congregation, and in 1869, when the new church was endowed, a new school was opened in the old chapel, which became the Todmorden Unitarian Sunday School. The old chapel was further extended and modernised in later years. A stone over the entrance reads:

"To the memory of Samuel, John and Joshua Fielden;
constant benefactors of the Unitarian Church and
School this stone was laid by Salfred Steintha
June 17th 1899."

Today the Sunday School is a workshop, yet another chapel building fallen to the ravages of today's unbelieving consumer society. In the 19th century both family and community life was centred on the chapel — today's urban man dedicates his spare time to TV. The material has replaced the spiritual, and in thousands of demolished or secularised chapels all over the region we are witnessing the "Fall of Zion". Today's society, living in the shadow of nuclear annihilation, sees no tomorrow, and it is hardly surprising to find that the solid faith and confidence in the future enjoyed by our Victorian forebears is singularly lacking today.

Chapels have now become workshops, recording studios, offices. There has even been a recent attempt to turn one into a witches' temple, and a century ago this would not only have been impossible but inconceivable! Today we are no longer subject to the tyrannical restrictions that were imposed on us by the blinkered guardians of Christian morality, but equally we are no longer able to enjoy the strength, fellowship and confidence that they took so much for granted. In rejecting the bad, alas, we have also rejected that which was good.

Before leaving the Sunday School yard take a look at the grave of James Graham, blacksmith of Dobroyd, whose headstone bears the following inscription:

"JAMES GRAHAM of DOBROYD, Todmorden.
Born March 18th 1837
Died February 12th 1876.

My sledge and hammer lay reclined
my bellows too have lost their wind
my fires extinguished and my forge decayed
my vice now in the dust is laid.
My iron and my coals are gone,
my nails are drove, my work is done
my fire dried corpse lies here at rest
my soul is waiting to be blest! "

From the graveyard descend steps to:-

The Golden Lion Inn

One of the older local hostelries, the Golden Lion has witnessed much of Todmorden's history. Situated in the old township of Langfield, it has an old drainpipe bearing the date 1789 on its rainwater head. An old coaching inn, it was very important in the days of turnpikes — the turnpike came to Todmorden in 1750 — when its innkeeper was both postmaster and coach proprietor. Both the 'Shuttle' and 'Perseverance' stagecoaches called here on their way to Halifax. The Golden Lion was the scene of many gatherings of local importance. It was for many years the meeting place of the Freeholders of Langfield Common, and as such was greatly involved with both the building and later re-building of Stoodley Pike Monument.

The Conservative Club

Across the square from the Golden Lion stands the Conservative Club. This was originally opened in 1880 as the Fielden Hotel and Coffee Tavern, and was, in its day, a stand for temperance in an area rich in taverns and hard drinking. It was built through the generosity of John Fielden J.P. of Dobroyd Castle. Closing its doors in April 1913, it reopened afterwards as a Conservative Club, the function it retains to this day. Outside it stood the statue of 'Honest John' Fielden, which is now situated in Centre Vale Park, at the very end of our journey.

From Fielden Square we pass through the heart of Todmorden to Centre Vale Park and the end of the Fielden Trail. By now, your feet will be telling you that you have nothing left to prove after having walked 99% of the route. "What is the point of walking this extra distance into Centre Vale Park?", you will be saying. You will have to walk back into the town centre when you've been there anyway! Well, if that's how you feel you can go home now, but if you'll bear with me, I'm sure that you will find the extra bit of walking required to complete the Fielden Trail quite worthwhile — there are still some stories left to be told and some ends to tie up.

From the Conservative Club follow the main road towards the centre of Todmorden. After crossing the canal turn left up Hall Street to the grounds of Todmorden Hall. The Fielden Trail passes the front of the house to emerge into Rise Lane on the other side.

Todmorden Hall

This magnificent house, formerly a Post Office and now used as a restaurant, stands at the very hub of Todmorden's history. The present hall was rebuilt in 1603 by Saville Radcliffe, whose family had lived there for several generations. It was a gentleman's house, built (by local standards) in the grandest possible style and up to the 1700s it was the very heart of Todmorden, which at that time was little more than the Hall, the Church, and a few cottages. Todmorden was unusual in those days; a small valley community, rare in a district where almost all the local population lived at a higher level on the surrounding hillsides. The main arteries of communication also tended to avoid the valleys in those times; so Todmorden was in many ways a quite untypical Pennine settlement.

By the 18th century Todmorden was growing, and the Hall passed into the hands of John Fielden, brother of Joshua (I) of Bottomley. John lived here from 1703 to 1734. Besides Joshua, John also had three other brothers, Nicholas and Samuel of Edge End, and Thomas of Hollingworth, all of them Quakers. In November 1707 John married Tamar Halstead of Erringden and they lived together at Todmorden Hall. John Fielden was a wealthy man: a prosperous woollen clothier who extended the Hall and built a "takkin' in shop" at the back, reached by a flight of external steps, which may still be seen. In the days of the handloom, weft and warp were given out to the weavers, and later the finished pieces were "taken in" here, hence the name. The weavers must have been a far cry from the gentry who would have visited the Hall in the days of the Radcliffes. John and Tamar Fielden must have been an industrious couple, for besides being deeply involved in the woollen trade they were also responsible for building the White Harte Inn which, like the Golden Lion, was witness to much of Todmorden's local history.

Tamar Fielden died on 8th January 1734 and was buried at Shoebroad. Her husband followed her on 20th May in the same year, having already made out his will in February. Their marriage had been childless, and John's estates, which also included Edge End, passed to his nephew Abraham, who in turn died at Todmorden Hall on 14th May 1779 aged 74. Like his uncle he was buried at Shoebroad. After this time the Hall passed from the Fieldens, later to become the residence of Mr. James Taylor Esq. the Magistrate, during which time the Hall suffered damage at the hands of the Anti Poor Law rioters. Now, in the 20th century, after a long career as a Post Office it has become a restaurant, and very attractive it is too, especially after a

Todmorden Hall.

long, tiring hike. (But I wouldn't go in there wearing hiking boots if I was you!)

Leave the hall grounds and turn left into Rise Lane, which leads to the station, and pass behind the church and the White Harte Inn. There was a temporary railway station here until 1844, but the present building dates from 1865. The massive goods yard retaining wall above the canal was built in 1881, and Fieldens were involved with much of this development. Both Thomas Fielden, 'Honest John's' brother, and his nephew Joshua were directors of the Lancashire and Yorkshire Railway. On 1st March 1841 Thomas Fielden complained about the practice of compelling 'waggon passengers' to arrive at the station ten minutes early. He was, it is said, a constant thorn in the flesh of the Railway Board's Chairman. Suggestions he made for improving the comfort of second and third class passengers were greeted with derision, and at some stations the following notice appeared:

"The Companies Servants are strongly ordered NOT to porter for waggon passengers . . ."

(Not even the railway companies, it seems, were spared the endless efforts of the Fieldens to improve the lot of the lower classes!).

The White Harte

Opposite the railway station stands the rear of the White Harte. The pub looks modern — and indeed it is, being built on the site of John and Tamar Fielden's original White Harte which was demolished in 1935. The original pub was built in 1720 and was also known as the New Inn. It was in front of this inn that the first Todmorden market was established in 1801; and later, between 1821 and 1851, when George Eccles and family occupied the inn, a court of Petty Sessions was established, and held upstairs in a room used by the local Freemasons for their affairs. As a result, when anyone had to appear in court, it was referred to as "goin' up Eccles' steps!"

In December 1830 'Honest John' addressed a meeting at Lumbutts which petitioned Lord Radnor and Henry Hunt in support of Parliamentary Reform, to which Earl Grey's new ministry was pledged. A month later, Fielden presided over another assembly, here at the White Harte, to found a "Political Union". Thereafter the Todmorden men joined their fellows in a network of Political Unions dedicated to Parliamentary Reform. Their good faith was rewarded, and in 1832, 350 reformers held a banquet to celebrate the passing of the Reform Bill, with John Fielden in the chair. A free meal was also provided for 3,000 of Fielden's workers at his own expense. As a result of this reform 'Honest John' was elected first ever M.P. for Oldham, and embarked upon his campaign to secure for the oppressed operatives of the northern mills a Ten Hours Bill. Here, at the White Harte an important chapter in the annals of English social history was begun.

Beyond the White Harte bear left, and follow the route under the viaduct and up 50 steps (Ridge Steps) to emerge on the 'Lover's Walk'. Soon terraced housing and Christ Church (scene of dreadful murders in 1868) appear on the right. Continue onwards, into Buckley Wood to arrive at the site of:-

Carr Laithe

Here at Carr Laithe in Buckley Wood once stood a farmhouse which was the setting for a romantic but rather sad episode in our "Fielden Saga". It was the home of John Stansfield, a poor farmer whose daughter Ruth was courted and married by John Fielden J.P. of Dobroyd Castle, 'Honest John's' second son. It was a classic "rags-to-riches-cum-Cinderella" story. When he and Ruth met she was a mere weaver at Waterside. He sent her away to be educated, but alas, she could never adapt to the Fielden's by now aristocratic lifestyle. She died, an alcoholic, on 6th February 1877 at the age of 50, and is buried at the Unitarian Chapel. In the same year John Fielden remarried, taking as his second wife Ellen, the daughter of the Revd. Richard Mallinson of Arkholme in Lancashire. John Fielden J.P. is buried, as we have already mentioned, at Grimston Park near Leeds. Perhaps it is from this story that the Lover's Walk derives its name? It would certainly be nice to think so.

From Carr Laithe follow the path, right, down into Centre Vale Park. Centre Vale Park is the site of the final "Fielden Mansion" to be visited on our route. Centre Vale was the first 'great' house of the Fielden family; a Georgian styled mansion which was the residence of 'Honest John' Fielden in later life, after he had sold Dawson Weir. (By the 1840's Dawson Weir was in the hands of the Holt family.) It ultimately became the residence of his eldest son, Samuel Fielden, until his death in 1889, after which his wife, Sarah Jane lived there until her death in 1910. In the Great War the house became a military hospital, and was eventually purchased, along with its estate of 75 acres, by Todmorden Corporation; who bought it from Samuel's son, John Ashton Fielden, for the sum of £10,547.

Between the wars the house was utilised as a museum, which housed fossils, butterflies, birds and relics of local prehistory. The Todmorden Historical Rooms were closed in 1947 because of dry rot, and the house was finally demolished in 1953. All that remains today is the park and a few of the old mansion's outbuildings. Part of the site now contains a war memorial and a garden of remembrance.

Centre Vale Park is the scene of an annual summer gala, and the 1984 gala saw the staging of the Battle of Gettysburg by one of those societies of enthusiasts, who delight in re-creating great military conflicts of the past. It was a spectacular event. The smoke of carbines and the roar of cannons could be seen, heard, (and felt) all over the valley. As I stood there, feeling the ground shaking beneath my feet as the guns roared, I wondered if anyone had realised the curious relevance of this event to the real life history of Todmorden; for the cannons of Gettysburg closed the mills of Todmorden and brought a hardship every bit as great as that endured by the Confederacy when Sherman began his famous "march to the sea".

From the very outset the whole of Lancashire's textile industry had been dependent upon an uninterrupted supply of imported raw cotton, and with the onset of the American Civil War in 1861, and the North's subsequent blockade of the Confederacy, the supply of cotton from the South began to steadily dry up. This caused widespread distress in the cotton manufacturing areas of Lancashire. A wave of speculation on the Liverpool Cotton Exchange made prices soar, and cotton was even taken from mills to be re-sold. At the same time the employers took advantage of the Cotton Famine to force down wages to as little as 4s and 5s a week. Soon, however, mills had closed down all over Lancashire and jobless operatives flooded the Unions demanding relief. In 1861 the census population of the Todmorden Union was 29,727 and the rateable assessment for the poor rate £89,696.

In order to help the various Boards of Guardians to cope with the distress the Union Relief Act was passed in 1862. This gave special powers, by which the public authorities could at once undertake a programme of public works, making roads, enlarging reservoirs, and cleaning out river beds. The Fielden brothers helped by employing men on road mending and making schemes. In connection with this work there were 3,000 suits of clothing and 300 pairs of watertight boots distributed. In 1863, when Fieldens were shut down for 9 months the employees were paid half their usual wages, and were given work cleaning the machines and reclaiming wastelands. The Todmorden Relief Fund Committee met in rooms at Dale Street while the Cotton Famine lasted, with John Fielden J.P. as its chairman. Work was found in other trades, and a sewing school established where girls could earn 6d a day for a five day week. Cheques to shop-keepers, payable in provisions or goods, were issued to those in the most urgent need.

All the mills in Todmorden were at a standstill; the only cotton available being Indian cotton, known as Shurat. This inferior cotton was notorious among cotton spinners for being 'bad' work. As one Todmorden operative put it — "we were fit for naught but to goa t't'bed when we'd done wi' it!". Even a generation later the word 'Shurat' was used in Lancashire as a synonym for 'rubbish'. A verse from a contemporary ballad, dating from the time of the 'Famine', and written by Samuel Laycock, who was a power loom weaver of Stalybridge, echoes the sentiment which must have been felt by the depressed and destitute operatives of Todmorden:

"Oh dear if yon Yankees could only just see
heaw they're clemmin' an' starvin' poor weavers loike me,
Aw think they'd sooin settle their bother and strive,
to send us some cotton to keep us alive.
Come give us a lift, yo' 'at han owt to give
an' help yo'r poor brothers an' sisters to live,
be kind an' be tender to th' needy and poor,
an' we'll promise when t'toimes mend
we'll ax yo' no moor . . ."

(Shurat Weaver's Song)

John Fielden's Statue (Terminus Absolute!)

Now, at last, we are approaching the end of the Fielden Trail. By a clump of rhododendrons, a little path from Carr Laithe meets another path coming up from the left. Turn sharp left and pass under trees to John Fielden's statue, which stands at a junction of park paths, near an aviary.

'Honest John's' statue has moved around a bit since it was unveiled at Todmorden on a blustery April day in 1875. Made by J. H. Foley in 1863, it stood originally by the western side of the Town Hall until 1890, when it was removed to Fielden Square and erected outside the present Conservative Club. It was moved to its present position in Centre Vale Park in 1938, and today there is talk of returning it to Fielden Square once again. The statue was unveiled by Lord John

Manners, who "tried to persuade Joshua Fielden (who was M.P. for Eastern Division W.R. Yorkshire) to let me say something handsome of Shaftesbury, but found, if I did, that he would break out in abuse!" The Fieldens had never forgiven Lord Shaftesbury (Ashley) for his "treason" in accepting Grey's compromise Factory Act in 1850. Even the commemoration of the old radical was not peaceful!

John Fielden must have cut a strange figure when he first took his seat in the re-organised Parliament of 1832. Tall and awkward, he spoke in a thick northern accent, in a voice which was barely audible; yet his sincerity and dedication more than made up for his shortcomings as an orator.

Fielden soon established himself as the leader of northern opposition to the hated 1834 Poor Law, and as chief promulgator of the Ten Hours Act, to limit hours of labour in factories and mines, towards which end he campaigned, collected evidence and spent thousands of pounds. To his friends he became known as 'Honest John' while his enemies dubbed him "The Self-Regulating Mule" on account of his refusal to compromise on matters of conscience. No doubt this quality led to the rift with Shaftesbury, who, although he shared Fielden's aims, was quite unlike him in background or temperament. Ashley Cooper could not stomach Fielden's Chartism, and together, the sensitive, aristocratic Shaftesbury and the radical, gritty millmaster must have made a strange pair!

In 1847, after an uphill struggle, the Ten Hours Movement's agitation succeeded, and Fielden was able to steer the Bill through Parliament. Yet at the end of 1847 Fielden must have had mixed feelings, for his political triumph was quickly followed by the collapse of his parliamentary career. In his opposition to the highly popular Anti Corn Law League, led by Bright, he lost many of his friends in Parliament, and in the hustings of that same year, 1847, he lost his seat to the Tories, who had rigged the election by threatening the livelihoods of voters. Losing his seat probably deprived him of his raison d'être, for within two years he was dead.

Back in 1847 Fielden addressed a rally in Oldham of his supporters, where he made what was to be his farewell speech. Towards the end of it, he uttered the following words:

"I have served you faithfully for 14 years. I never bought you . . . I never sold you. I have tried all I could to endeavour to do something calculated to make you more comfortable and more happy — and having succeeded in that object which I had so much at heart, I can now well afford to go out to grass . . ."

So here we are, tired and footsore, at the end of our Fielden Trail.

Before you stands the frail figure of 'Honest John' cast in bronze; he stares benevolently across the park to where the children play. Foley made his likeness well. 'Honest John' looks like he could step off his pedestal and shake your hand, so lifelike is his expression! In his right hand he grasps that Ten Hours Bill which he struggled so single-mindedly to obtain. This was 'Honest John's' supreme achievement, the effect of which is well summed up in the words of Moses Heap, a Rossendale spinner:

"For a while we did not know how to pass our time away. Before, it had been all bed and work, now, in place of 70 hours a week we had 55 and a half. It became a practice, mostly on Saturdays to play football and cricket, which we had never done before . . ."

Today 'Honest John's' statue watches over the park where local people still play football and cricket, enjoying the free time which John Fielden pioneered for them. Football and cricket, in his park! 'Honest John' would have liked that! Before we trudge back to Todmorden Bus Station, car park, chip shop, cafe or whatever, let me leave you with a few words that were written about this man, who has always been at the very heart of our Fielden quest, for without him, such a journey as this we have made would have neither point nor meaning. I will leave you with the following extract from R. G. Gammage's book 'The History of the Chartist Movement' in which he says of 'Honest John' Fielden:

"That gentleman was known as the successor to the principles and honour of the immortal Cobbett, and was deservedly popular for the warm and unceasing interest he had taken in the fate of the industrial millions. No man, according to his powers, had been a more strenuous opponent of the new Poor Law, and against the police system he had taken an equally decided stand. But what most gained for him the heartfelt affection of the working class, was the position which he, a rich manufacturer, had taken as the unqualified denouncer of factory oppression. There was scarcely a measure he was not prepared to adopt in order to protect the people from the grasping 'cottonocracy'. A Ten Hours Bill was the object of his constant advocacy, and it was he who succeeded at last in carrying that measure through the legislature . . . The man, standing apart from the generality of his class, ventured in whatever way to plead the claims of suffering humanity against wealth and power.

Fielden had shown himself to be something more than a mere factory reformer, he had everywhere declared himself to be the advocate of Universal Suffrage. He did not merely profess himself willing to protect the people against agression, but, by striving to arm them with the Vote, he manifested a desire to give them the opportunity of protecting themselves. In this he proved himself to be something better than a mere 'humanity monger' aping philanthropy for the purpose of catching a little popularity. As a speaker, he was far from being effective, his sincerity rather than his oratory, gave him force. He was ever earnest, disdaining to strive after mere effect, but courageously plodding on in his own humble and unpretending way towards the attainment of his object. He has now gone to the tomb of his fathers, peace rest his ashes! The sun has seldom shone over a better man than John Fielden."

Postscript

We have now reached the end of the Fielden Trail. We have not, however, reached the end of the Fielden family. Our 'History' effectively ends with the deaths of 'Honest John's' last remaining sons; but the Fieldens did not die out — children were plentiful and the line continued, along with all the other, less eminent branches of the Fielden family to be found in the Upper Calder Valley, and elsewhere. Fieldens are as plentiful today as they were a century ago, and the only reason our trail ends where it does, is because it concentrates on 'Honest John's' line, which, after the deaths of Sam, John and Joshua came to be less and less associated with Todmorden and the Upper Calder Valley. Their mansions and parks remain, but Fieldens no longer live in them. In 1959 the Cotton Industry Act compensated employers for getting rid of old machinery. More than 12 million spindles and nearly 105,000 looms were scrapped and the workforce fell by 30% in 2 years. Trade had been declining since the 1930s, and by 1958 Britain had become a net importer of cotton goods for the first time since the 18th century! Cheap, foreign cloth was forcing mill closures, (in the 1960s and '70s almost one a week). The Fieldens' cotton empire, being one of the biggest, was one of the first to collapse, and by the 1960s Fieldens' cotton mills had shut down for good.

The family remains: John Fielden of Grimston Park, Tadcaster, great, great, grandson of 'Honest John' was recorded as being head of the family in 1968. His great aunt Ellen died in 1956 aged 100, his great aunt Edith married Sir John Mackintosh McLeod, 1st Bt. His great uncle Edward, who lived at Dobroyd Castle was M.P. for S.E. Lancashire 1886-92 and 1895-7. All these were Joshua Fielden of Stansfield Hall's children. Lionel Fielden, another relative, was Director of Talks BBC 1927-35 and Controller of Broadcasting in India 1935-40. A playwright, he is the author of Beggar My Neighbour (1943) and The Natural Bent (1960). His recreation is given in 'Who's Who' as "trying to avoid being organised."

These of course are not the only Fieldens. Other branches of the family abound, and any glance at the local 'phone book will affirm that Fielden is a fairly common name in the Todmorden area. There are firms of that name in Todmorden, and at least one of them is still associated with the textile business. (Fielden Rigg Ltd, Sizers, of Dancroft and Bridge Mills, Todmorden). There is a Fielden on the local Council, and there are many, many, lesser lights.

As this story ends the saga of the Fieldens continues. I wonder what Nicholas and Christobel Fielden's four sons, the origin of all the Fieldens in the Upper Calder Valley, would have made of the last words in this story, which I saw chalked on a wall opposite the Council Offices in Hebden Bridge, in July 1984:

"COLIN FIELDEN IS FIT
O.K. ? "

Bibliograpby

Ashworth, T. Edwin. *A fragment of Todmorden History.* (Pamphlet.)
Aspin, Chris. *The Cotton Industry.* Shire Books, 1981.
Birch, Roger. *A Way of Life.* E J Morton, Manchester 1972.
Birch, Roger. *Todmorden Album.* Woodland Press, Todmorden 1983.
Bewes, Richard. *John Wesley's England.* Hodder & Stoughton, London 1981.
Borough Guide to Todmorden. J W Crowther, Newsagent & Stationer. (Pamphlet.)
Calderdale Way Association. *The Calderdale Way.* 1978.
Dewhirst, Ian. *Yorkshire Through the Years.* Batsford, London 1975.
Fielden, John. *The Curse of the Factory System.* Frank Cass & Co., London. Republished 1969 with an introduction by J T Ward, University of Strathclyde.
Fishwick, Henry, FSA. *A Genealogical Memorial of the Family of Fielden of Todmorden.* Privately printed Mitchell & Hughes, London, 1894.
Green, J R. *A Short History of the English People.* Macmillan, London 1919.
Holden. *A Short History of Todmorden.* Published by Manchester University, 1912.
Jarratt, J F. *'Honest John': A Brief Biography of John Fielden MP.* (Unpublished manuscript.)
Kelly's Post Office Directory of the West Riding of Yorkshire, 1861.
Marshal, John. *The Lancashire and Yorkshire Railway Volume One.* David & Charles, London 1969.
Methuen. *English Historical Documents 1815-70.* Methuen, London 1964.
Murtagh, M. *New Ways, New Cloths.* Pennine Heritage Network, Hebden Bridge 1982.
Newell, Abraham. *A Hillside View of Industry.* Newell, 1925.
Palmer, A. *A Touch on the Times: Songs of Social Change.* Penguin, London 1974.
Pevsner, N. *The Buildings of England: The Yorkshire West Riding.* Penguin, London 1959.

Porter, John. *The Making of the Central Pennines*. Moorland Publishing Co., Buxton 1980.

Round, Philip. *Heptonstall History Trail*. Calder Civic Trust, Heptonstall 1972.

Ramshaw, *Concerning Todmorden Parish*. F Lee, Todmorden 1911.

Savage, E M. *The Development of Todmorden from 1700 to 1896*. Todmorden Antiquarian Society (undated).

Savage, E M. *Stoodley Pike*. Todmorden Antiquarian Society, 1974.

Tenen, I, MA. *This England 1714-1940*. Macmillan, London 1955.

Thompson, E P. *The Making of the English Working Class*. Victor Gollancz, London 1963.

Todmorden and Hebden Bridge Historical Almanacks, 1865-1913.

Todmorden Guide.

Todmorden Library Journals.

Todmorden's 75th Anniversary. (Booklet.)

Travis, John. *Notes Historical and Biographical. Mainly of Todmorden and District*. E Wrigley, Todmorden 1896.

Travis, John. *Historical Notes and Personal Reminiscences.*

Travis, John. *Some Old Walsden Families*. Fletcher Printers, Birks Terrace 1891.

Unitarian Social Reformers 2: John Fielden. Lindsey Press, London 1923.

Wightman. *Pennine Panorama*. Gerrard Publishers, Nelson, Lancs 1969.

Contemporary Material

An Account of the Poor Law Riots at Todmorden, 21st November 1938. (Pamphlet).

Funeral of Mr Fielden. Ashton Chronicle, 1849. (News Article).

Obituary to Thomas Fielden. Born 11th December 1790, Died 7th December 1869. From the Manchester Courier 21st December 1869. J Bentley Printers, Todmorden. (Pamphlet.)

The Ten Hours Bill. To the Factory Operatives of Great Britain and Ireland. Published by the Lancashire Central Short Time Committee, July 1844. (Pamphlet.)

The Ten Hours Bill. Report of the proceedings of the delegates from the operatives of Lancashire and Yorkshire sent by the factory workers of those counties to assist Lord Ashley MP in promoting the Ten Hours Bill, with the speech of John Fielden M.P. in the House of Commons on 18th March. Published Manchester 1844.

'Great Demonstration' at Oldham in honour of John Fielden and J M Cobbett Esq., and in commemoration of the passing of the Ten Hours Bill on Tuesday August 31st 1847. The Oldham Monthly Rememberance and Working Man's Friend, printed Manchester 1847.
Letters of Mary Fielden 1836-1841. (Manuscript.)
Letter of Sam Fielden, 1841. (Manuscript.)

Additional Material

Breakell, Ruth. *Caring and Sharing.* Pennine Heritage Network, Hebden Bridge 1982.
Gammage, R G. *History of the Chartist Movement.* F Cass, London 1897. (Reprinted in 1969 by Merlin Press.)
Gregg, Pauline. *A Social and Economic History of Britain.* Harrap, London 1973.
Jones, David. *Chartism and the Chartit.* Penguin, London 1975.
Parry, Keith. *Trans-Pennine Heritage.* David & Charles, London 1981.
Slack, Margaret. *Portrait of West Yorkshire.* Robert Hale, London 1984.
Speed, P F. *Social Problems of the Industrial Revolution.* Wheaton, Exeter 1975.

Index